# *Desserts*

## PUDDINGS & ICES

**MURDOCH BOOKS**®
Sydney • London • Vancouver • New York

# Contents

# Sweet Temptations

*F*east your eyes and tempt your tastebuds with our exciting collection of desserts, ranging from the quickest fruit salad to crisp meringues, creamy mousses and fluffy soufflés. A dessert, no matter how simple or spectacular, provides the finishing touch to any meal and is the one course that everyone eagerly awaits. With just a little planning and some decoration, we show you how to make the dessert course the easiest and most impressive part of the meal.

Desserts are not just for dinner parties. More often than not, the family looks forward to a sweet treat to finish a meal. Family desserts are especially enjoyable because they include all the favourites such as Rhubarb Crumble, Queen of Puddings and Bread and Butter Pudding (see recipes). Not only are they moreish but they provide the opportunity of using up excess fruit and ingredients which often leads to new dishes being created.

## INSTANT DESSERTS

Sometimes the temptation for a dessert is a spur of the moment decision and with a few ingredients stacked away in the pantry you can create a number of delicious, interesting sweets. Try dried fruit soaked in sherry, or coconut cream melted into natural yoghurt as a quick sauce for fruit, or natural yoghurt pureed with dried apricots, spiced with cinnamon and topped with crushed pistachios.

## THE PANTRY SHELF SHOPPING LIST

NUTS: Pistachio, walnuts, almonds, pecans, hazelnuts
DRIED FRUIT: Apricots, prunes, bananas, apples, sultanas, dates, coconut, prunes
SPICES: Cinnamon, cloves, nutmeg, mixed spice
ASSORTED INGREDIENTS: Dark chocolate, white chocolate, caster sugar, brown sugar, icing sugar, honey, natural yoghurt, ice cream, coconut cream, canned fruit, marshmallows, rose water, frozen filo and puff pastry, golden syrup, treacle.

## PRODUCE

When buying fruit for a dessert, especially if it is to be served raw, buy only the best quality. Feel the fruit and select only firm, plump produce, avoiding any with bruised or discoloured skin. Avoid shrivelled produce or fruit that will be over-ripe by the time you want to serve it. Be adventurous: if a new fruit appears on the market, buy a small quantity of it and highlight it in a dish for the family, if it's a success then incorporate it into your repertoire for entertaining.

Take advantage of surplus fruit which is often available at low prices. Cook it in wine with spices such as cloves or cinnamon; poach it in a sugar syrup or puree it to make a fruit sauce. Any excess can be frozen and used later in a jelly, sorbet, ice cream or mousse.

## DECORATIONS

A few easy decorations can turn a simple dessert into a spectacular course and, for the occasional mishap, hide a multitude of sins!

Feature one of the ingredients in the dessert as part of the decoration. With a citrus dessert for example, poach or caramelise some of the rind and sprinkle it over the finished dish. Cut fruit such as grapefruit, pineapple, orange or kiwi fruit so that the shell can be saved and used as a serving dish.

Jam glaze brushed over a fruit tart not only enhances the colour and gives it a shiny finish but also prevents the fruit from drying out.

Alternatively, dip whole pieces of fruit, such as strawberries, mandarin segments or grapes first into a sugar syrup, dust with caster sugar for a frosted effect, then use them to decorate.

Chocolate is useful for decorating desserts as it is so easy to store and gives a number of different decorative finishes or coatings. For a quick garnish, shave chocolate off the block with a potato peeler or cut into long flakes to serve with ice cream. Paint melted chocolate onto leaves, then peel away the leaf leaving a perfect impression which can be used on

gateaux, mousses or as a plate garnish. Coat cupcake moulds with chocolate, then peel away the casing and fill the cups with fresh fruit which has also been dipped in chocolate. This can either be served with coffee or topped with piped cream for a quick yet effective dessert.

The secret of successful desserts is to work with the ingredients you have or with produce in season, and adapt to fit the occasion. Anticipation is on your side, and family and friends will look forward to your experiments and discoveries with enthusiasm and delight.

Plates from Waterford Wedgwood, fabric from I Redelman and Son

# Warm and Cosy Puddings

*P*uddings evoke a wonderfully warm atmosphere around a dining table. Their prepare-ahead nature means that all of the hard work is done before the meal begins, leaving you free to enjoy the company of your friends and family while your dessert bubbles merrily on.

# The Secrets of Steaming the Perfect Pudding

Cooking a perfect pudding is easy. Follow the steps below to ensure you have a perfect pudding every time.

THE PUDDING BASIN:

- A heatproof pudding basin is ideal for cooking puddings in, although other tins such as small cake tins, brioche tins or small heatproof souffle dishes or ramekins can also be used.
- Before preparing the pudding mixture, place the pudding basin inside the saucepan you are using and check to see that there is at least 2.5 cm (1 in) space between the basin and the saucepan. Circulation of steam is vital during cooking.

THE ESSENTIAL PREPARATION:

- Place two pieces of greased paper in the base of the pudding basin to ensure the pudding will slide from the basin easily.
- Puddings rise during cooking so do not fill the basin more than two-thirds full.

WRAPPING IT UP:

- The correct way to cover a pudding is to first place a greased and pleated piece of paper over the pudding to prevent it from becoming soggy. Follow this with a pleated piece of foil. Secure both layers tightly with string. Tie another piece of string to form a handle so that you can lift the pudding easily to and from the saucepan.

... AND PLENTY OF BOILING WATER:

- Have the saucepan three-quarters full of water that is boiling, before placing the pudding in the saucepan to cook.

*Pictured on previous pages: Hazelnut Praline Pudding (page 11), Sticky Date Pudding (page 19), Caramelised Pear Bread Pudding (page 12)*

- The water should always be at least half-way up the sides of the basin or tin. Make sure that the water is already boiling before lowering the pudding into the saucepan. It is also very important to ensure that the water continues to boil for the complete cooking time.
- Check water level during cooking—do not let the pudding boil dry. Top up the water, with boiling water if necessary.
- Always have a tight fitting lid on the saucepan so that the steam cannot escape.

## WHAT WENT WRONG?

IF THE PUDDING IS TOO DENSE, HEAVY AND SOGGY:

- Not enough raising agent has been used. Use either a chemical, such as baking powder, or incorporate air by beating and folding.
- The water was allowed to go off the boil.

IF THE PUDDING STICKS TO THE BASIN OR TIN:

- The base was not lined with paper.
- The basin was not greased or not greased enough.
- The pudding may be undercooked.

IF THE PUDDING IS NOT COOKED IN THE CENTRE:

- The pudding may have been allowed to go off the boil.
- The pudding was not cooked for long enough.

IF THE PUDDING HAS A DRY OR BURNT BASE:

- The temperature may have been too high.
- The pudding basin may have a thin base. Next time, place an upturned saucer in the base of the saucepan.

# LEMON PUDDING

**PUDDING**

 90 g (3 oz) butter

 125 g (4 oz) sugar

 2 eggs, lightly beaten

 2 tablespoons lemon marmalade

 185 g (6 oz) self-raising flour

 ⅓ cup (80 ml/2¾ fl oz)
  buttermilk

**SAUCE**

 125 g (4 oz) lemon marmalade

 2 tablespoons sugar

 1 cup (250 ml/8 fl oz) water

 3 teaspoons grated lemon rind

To Make Pudding: Beat butter and sugar in a bowl until light and fluffy. Beat in eggs and marmalade. Fold through flour and buttermilk.

Pour into a greased 6 cup (1.5 litre/48 fl oz) pudding steamer. Cover with greased paper. Secure with lid or aluminium foil. Place pudding in a large saucepan of simmering water. Cover and cook for 1½ hours.

To Make Sauce: Simmer marmalade, sugar, water and rind in a small saucepan for 10 minutes or until sauce thickens. Turn pudding onto a serving plate. Serve with sauce.

**SERVES 8**

# SAGO PUDDING

 90 g (3 oz) sago

 1 cup (250 ml/8 fl oz) milk

 60 g (2 oz) brown sugar

*Lemon Pudding*

 1 tablespoon honey

 1 teaspoon orange zest

 60 g (2 oz) fresh breadcrumbs

Cover sago with cold water and soak overnight.

Preheat oven to 180°C (350°F). Grease four ½ cup (125 ml/4 fl oz) ramekins.

Drain sago. Combine well in a bowl with milk, sugar, honey, zest and breadcrumbs.

Spoon mixture into ramekins. Cover with foil. Place ramekins in a baking dish half filled with water. Bake for 1 hour. Remove foil and serve.

**SERVES 4**

# TANGELO PUDDING WITH COCONUT ICE CREAM

## PUDDING

- 125 g (4 oz) butter
- 85 g (3 oz) caster sugar
- 2 eggs, separated
- 1 tablespoon grated tangelo rind
- 150 g (5 oz) self-raising flour
- ½ cup (125 ml/4 fl oz) milk
- 85 g (3 oz) desiccated coconut
- 1 tangelo, chopped, pith and seeds removed

## COCONUT ICE CREAM

- 4 cups (1 litre/32 fl oz) vanilla ice cream, softened
- 2 tablespoons grated tangelo rind
- 75 g (2½ oz) toasted shredded coconut

To Make Pudding: Beat butter and sugar in a bowl until light and creamy. Beat in egg yolks and rind. Fold through flour, milk, coconut and tangelo. Beat egg whites in another bowl until stiff peaks form. Fold through mixture.

Pour into a greased and double lined 18 cm (7 in) cake tin. Secure top with aluminium foil and string. Place in a large saucepan of simmering water, cover and cook for 2 hours 40 minutes or until set.

*Banana Butterscotch Pudding, Tangelo Pudding with Coconut Ice Cream*

To Make Coconut Ice Cream: Combine ice cream in a bowl with rind and coconut. Refreeze until required.

Serve pudding with scoops of coconut ice cream.

**SERVES 6**

# BANANA BUTTERSCOTCH PUDDING

### PUDDING

400 g (12½ oz) can sweetened condensed milk

60 g (2 oz) butter

1 teaspoon vanilla essence

½ cup (125 ml/4 fl oz) milk

220 g (7 oz) self-raising flour

3 tablespoons ground almonds

2 ripe bananas, mashed

### SAUCE

155 g (5 oz) brown sugar

1¾ cups (430 ml/14 fl oz) boiling water

Preheat oven to 180°C (350°F).

To Make Pudding: Stir condensed milk in a small saucepan over low heat for 10 minutes or until lightly golden. Stir in butter, vanilla and milk. Cook until butter melts.

In a bowl combine flour, almonds, bananas and milk mixture. Pour mixture into a greased 8 cup (2 litre/64 fl oz) ovenproof dish.

To Make Sauce: Sprinkle the pudding mixture in dish with brown sugar and carefully pour over boiling water.

Bake for 35 minutes or until top is cooked.

**SERVES 6**

# HAZELNUT PRALINE PUDDING

### PRALINE

125 g (4 oz) sugar

3 tablespoons boiling water

125 g (4 oz) hazelnuts

### PUDDING

125 g (4 oz) butter

4 eggs, separated

½ cup (125 ml/4 fl oz) milk

65 g (2 oz) hazelnuts, roasted and chopped

155 g (5 oz) choc chip cookies, crushed

2 tablespoons self-raising flour

To Make Praline: Stir sugar and water in a small saucepan over low heat until sugar dissolves. Bring to the boil. Add hazelnuts and simmer until syrup is golden brown. Pour onto a greased oven tray. Cool and set. Break into pieces. Process in the food processor until very finely chopped.

Preheat oven to 190°C (375°F).

To Make Pudding: Beat butter and praline in a bowl until light and fluffy. Beat in egg yolks and milk. Fold through hazelnuts, crushed cookies and flour. Beat egg whites in a bowl until stiff peaks form. Fold through mixture. Pour mixture into a greased kugelhopf tin or fluted cake tin. Bake for 50 minutes or until cooked. Serve with Praline Custard (see page 20).

**SERVES 6**

# MOCHA PUDDING WITH FUDGE SAUCE

A great pudding for those cold raining nights. A mocha sponge top conceals a rich fudge sauce.

## PUDDING

- 125 g (4 oz) demerara sugar
- 125 g (4 oz) self-raising flour
- ½ teaspoon baking powder
- 60 g (2 oz) butter, chopped
- 1½ tablespoons instant coffee powder
- 150 ml (5 fl oz) milk
- 2 tablespoons cocoa powder

## FUDGE SAUCE

- 225 g (7½ oz) demerara sugar
- 75 g (2½ oz) cocoa powder
- 200 ml (7 fl oz) milk
- 225 ml (7½ fl oz) cream

Preheat oven to 180°C (350°F).

To Make Pudding: Place sugar, flour and baking powder in a bowl. Combine butter, coffee, milk and cocoa in a small saucepan and stir over low heat until smooth.

Pour into dry ingredients. Mix well to combine. Pour mixture into a greased, medium sized ovenproof dish.

To Make Fudge Sauce: Evenly sprinkle sugar and cocoa over mixture in dish. Pour over combined milk and cream.

Bake for 1 hour. Serve in scoops with the sauce from the bottom of the dish. Add ice cream if desired.

SERVES 6

# CARAMELISED PEAR BREAD PUDDING

- 60 g (2 oz) butter
- 60 g (2 oz) brown sugar
- 3 pears, peeled and sliced
- 12 slices bread, crusts removed
- 125 g (4 oz) butter, softened
- 250 g (8 oz) sultanas
- 3 eggs, lightly beaten
- 250 g (8 oz) sugar
- 300 ml (10 fl oz) cream
- 300 ml (10 fl oz) milk
- ½ teaspoon ground nutmeg
- ½ teaspoon ground cinnamon

Preheat oven to 180°C (350°F).

Heat butter in a frying pan. Add brown sugar, stirring over low heat until sugar dissolves. Add pear slices and cook until golden.

Remove pears from pan. Pour remaining caramel into the base of a greased 12 x 25 cm (5 x 10 in) loaf tin. Arrange one-third of the pears over the caramel.

Spread bread with butter. Place a layer of bread over pears, cutting shape to fit. Sprinkle bread with one-third of the sultanas.

Repeat layers and finish with a layer of bread. Place eggs, sugar, cream, milk, nutmeg and cinnamon in a bowl. Whisk to combine. Pour over bread and stand for 20 minutes.

Bake for 30 minutes or until set.

Stand for 5 minutes. Invert onto a serving dish and serve in slices.

SERVES 8 TO 10

# CHOCOLATE BROWNIE SOUFFLE

- caster sugar
- 85 g (3 oz) butter
- 125 g (4 oz) milk chocolate, chopped
- 100 g (3½ oz) sugar
- 3 egg yolks
- 1 teaspoon vanilla essence
- 3 tablespoons self-raising flour
- 4 egg whites
- thick cream and chocolate shavings

Preheat oven to 230°C (450°F).

Grease four 1 cup (250 ml/8 fl oz) ramekins. Sprinkle the base and sides with caster sugar.

Stir butter and chocolate in a bowl over a saucepan of simmering water until smooth. Stir through half the sugar, with the egg yolks, vanilla and flour. Remove from heat.

Beat egg whites in a bowl until stiff peaks form. Gradually add remaining sugar, beating until thick and glossy. Fold egg whites through chocolate mixture. Spoon into ramekins.

Bake for 5 minutes. Reduce temperature to 200°C (400°F). Bake for a further 10 minutes. The soufflés should be soft in the middle. Serve with thick cream and chocolate shavings.

SERVES 4

---

**MELTING CHOCOLATE**

When melting chocolate ensure that the bowl is suspended over, not in, the simmering not boiling water. If the temperature is too hot it can give the chocolate a bitter taste.

---

*Chocolate Brownie Soufflé*

# RICH FRUIT PUDDING

400 g (12½ oz) mixed sultanas, currants and raisins

100 g (3½ oz) pitted prunes, chopped

55 g (2 oz) mixed peel

125 g (4 oz) almonds, finely chopped

1 cup (250 ml/8 fl oz) orange juice

1 tablespoon grated lemon rind

3 tablespoons rum or brandy

125 g (4 oz) butter

90 g (3 oz) brown sugar

2 eggs, lightly beaten

90 g (3 oz) self-raising flour

155 g (5 oz) soft fresh breadcrumbs

1 teaspoon ground mixed spice

1 teaspoon ground cinnamon

1 apple, grated

2 carrots, grated

Brandy Custard (see recipe, page 21)

In a large bowl, mix together dried fruit, prunes, mixed peel, almonds, orange juice, lemon rind and brandy. Stand overnight.

Beat butter and sugar in a bowl until light and creamy. Gradually add eggs, beating well. Fold through flour, breadcrumbs, spice, cinnamon, apple, carrots and fruit mixture. Cover and stand overnight.

Grease and double line the base of a 6 cup (1.5 litre/48 fl oz) pudding basin. Pour mixture into basin. Fit with a well sealing lid or cover with aluminium foil secured with string.

Place basin in a large saucepan of simmering water. Cover and simmer for 8 hours. Top up saucepan with boiling water as necessary. Allow

*Sweet Potato and Zucchini Pudding and Plum Pud*

pudding to cool. Store in a cool dry place.

To reheat, simmer in boiling water for 4 to 5 hours. Serve with Brandy Custard.

**SERVES 8 TO 10**

# SWEET POTATO AND ZUCCHINI PUDDING

350 g (11 oz) sweet potato, peeled and chopped

125 g (4 oz) zucchini, grated

1 tablespoon grated orange rind

½ cup (125 ml/4 fl oz) orange juice

55 g (2 oz) butter

100 g (3½ oz) brown sugar

3 eggs, separated

90 g (3 oz) self-raising flour

1 teaspoon cinnamon

Citrus Sauce (see recipe, page 20)

Cook sweet potato in a small amount of water until soft. Mash well. Mix with zucchini, orange rind and juice. Set aside.

Beat butter and sugar in a bowl until light and creamy. Add egg yolks, beating well. Fold through flour, cinnamon and sweet potato mixture. Beat egg whites in another bowl until stiff peaks form and fold through pudding mixture.

Pour mixture into a greased and double lined 6 cup (1.5 litre/ 48 fl oz) pudding basin. Secure with a tight fitting lid or aluminium foil and string.

Place in a saucepan of boiling water. Cover and cook for 1¾ hours. Invert onto a serving plate. Serve with Citrus Sauce.

**SERVES 4**

# CHERRY JANE

550 g (17 oz) cherries, stoned

grated rind and juice ½ lemon

150 g (5 oz) stale cake crumbs

40 g (1⅓ oz) butter, melted

250 g (8 oz) sugar

Preheat oven to 180°C (350°F).

Mix cherries with lemon rind and juice. Mix half the cake crumbs with melted butter. Grease a pie plate and cover base with a layer of cherries. Sprinkle with sugar and top with unbuttered crumbs. Repeat layers, topping finally with the buttered crumbs. Cover and bake for 45 minutes. Remove cover and bake further 15 minutes.

**SERVES 4**

# PLUM PUD

Fresh or canned plums can be used.

600 g (1¼ lb) plums, halved and stoned

2 tablespoons caster sugar

1 tablespoon grated lemon rind

125 g (4 oz) butter, melted

125 g (4 oz) ground almonds

125 g (4 oz) sugar

2 eggs, lightly beaten

150 ml (5 fl oz) milk

2 teaspoons vanilla essence

icing sugar

cream or ice cream

Preheat oven to 180°C (350°F).

Place plums in the base of a large ovenproof dish. Sprinkle with caster sugar and rind. Combine butter, almonds, sugar, eggs, milk and vanilla in a bowl. Spread over plums. Bake for 45 minutes or until set. Dust with icing sugar and serve with cream or ice cream.

**SERVES 6 TO 8**

# HONEY PUDDING WITH CINNAMON SYRUP

### PUDDING

> 125 g (4 oz) butter
>
> 60 g (2 oz) raw sugar
>
> 2 eggs, lightly beaten
>
> 125 g (4 oz) self-raising flour
>
> 1 teaspoon vanilla essence
>
> 4 tablespoons honey

### CINNAMON SYRUP

> 1 cup (250 ml/8 fl oz) water
>
> 2 cinnamon sticks
>
> 2 large pieces lemon rind
>
> 3 tablespoons honey

To Make Pudding: Beat butter and sugar in a bowl until light and creamy. Add eggs, beating well. Fold through flour and vanilla.

Grease a 4 cup (1 litre/32 fl oz) pudding basin. Place honey in basin and swirl to coat sides. Pour in mixture. Secure with a tight lid or aluminium foil and string.

Place in a saucepan of simmering water. Cover and cook for 1½ hours.

To Make Cinnamon Syrup: Simmer water, cinnamon, rind and honey in a small saucepan for 4 minutes or until thickened. Remove cinnamon and rind.

Invert pudding onto a plate and serve with syrup.

**SERVES 4 TO 6**

# STICKY FIG PUDDING

### PUDDING

> 150 g (5 oz) dried figs, chopped
>
> 150 ml (5 fl oz) boiling water
>
> 85 g (3 oz) butter
>
> 90 g (3 oz) brown sugar
>
> 1 egg
>
> 375 g (12 oz) self-raising flour

### TOPPING

> 85 g (3 oz) butter
>
> 175 g (5¾ oz) brown sugar
>
> 3 tablespoons thickened cream
>
> extra cream

Place figs and boiling water in a bowl. Set aside for 30 minutes.

To Make Topping: Stir butter, sugar and cream in a small saucepan until smooth. Bring to the boil and simmer for 3 minutes. Pour topping into the base of a greased 6 cup (1.5 litre/48 fl oz) pudding basin.

Beat butter and sugar in a bowl until light and creamy. Beat in egg. Fold through flour and fig mixture. Pour mixture carefully over topping.

Secure with a tight fitting lid or aluminium foil and string. Place in a saucepan of boiling water, cover and cook for 2 hours.

Invert pudding and serve with extra cream.

**SERVES 6**

*Honey Pudding with Cinnamon Syrup and Sticky Fig Pudding*

Whether you use a steamer or a saucepan, the water must be kept gently and constantly boiling throughout the cooking time. It should be topped up from time to time, to compensate for evaporation. The basin should be lightly greased with butter and no more than ⅔ full with the pudding mixture. It is a good idea to insert a disc of well-buttered greaseproof paper over the base of the basin before adding the pudding mixture. This will prevent the pudding sticking when it is turned out. If you follow these instructions and the recipes on the following pages you will turn out the most irresistibly tasty and nourishing winter desserts.

# QUEEN OF PUDDINGS

2½ cups (600 ml/20 fl oz) milk

165 g (5¼ oz) caster sugar

240 g (8 oz) cake crumbs

grated rind 2 lemons

2 eggs, separated

250 g (8 oz) apricot jam

Preheat oven to 180°C (350°F).

Heat milk and 55 g (2 oz) of sugar gently in a pan. Stir in cake crumbs and lemon rind, then remove from heat. Beat in egg yolks.

Pour half the mixture into a greased earthenware dish and bake for 30 minutes or until set.

Heat apricot jam in a saucepan and spread half over top of set custard. Top up dish with remaining egg yolk mixture and return to oven for 30 minutes or until set.

Cover top of pudding with rest of jam. Whisk egg whites with 55 g (2 oz) of remaining sugar until stiff.

Raise oven temperature to 190°C (375°F). Pile whisked meringue on pudding and sprinkle with remaining sugar.

Return to oven and bake for 5 minutes or until meringue is golden. Serve immediately.

**SERVES 6**

# PERSIMMON AND CURRANT PUDDING

180 g (6 oz) butter

375 g (12 oz) sugar

3 eggs, lightly beaten

pulp of 5 persimmons

3 teaspoons bicarbonate of soda

220 g (7 oz) currants

3 tablespoons orange liqueur (eg Cointreau)

1 teaspoon vanilla essence

185 g (6 oz) plain flour

Custard (see recipe, page 21)

Beat butter and sugar in a bowl until light and creamy. Add eggs, beating well.

Mix through persimmon pulp, bicarbonate of soda, currants, liqueur, vanilla and flour.

Pour mixture into a 10 cup (2.5 litre/80 fl oz) greased and double lined pudding basin. Secure with a tight fitting lid or aluminium foil and string.

Place in a large saucepan of boiling water. Cover and cook for 3 hours. Stand for 5 minutes before turning onto a serving plate. Serve in slices with Custard.

**SERVES 12**

# SPOTTED DICK

95 g (3 oz) fresh breadcrumbs

75 g (2½ oz) shredded suet

55 g (2 oz) caster sugar

110 g (3½ oz) currants, raisins or sultanas

95 g (3 oz) self-raising flour

pinch salt

⅓ cup (85 ml/3 fl oz) milk

pinch cinnamon, ginger or nutmeg (optional)

Place breadcrumbs, shredded suet, sugar and currants in a bowl. Sift in flour, salt and spices mix well. Make a well in the mixture and mix in milk, a little at a time, until you have a soft dough. Add more milk if needed.

Grease a 1 litre mould (or basin) — use a fluted one for a more attractive appearance. Spoon mixture into mould or basin and cover loosely with two thicknesses of greaseproof paper, or aluminium foil. Tie with string and make sure it is well-sealed.

Steam over boiling water for 1½ to 2 hours. Turn out mould and serve with hot custard or a fruit sauce.

**SERVES 4 TO 6**

# MARBLE PUDDING

2 eggs

220 g (7 oz) caster sugar

3 tablespoons vegetable oil

2 cups (500 ml/16 fl oz) milk

375 g (12 oz) self-raising flour

1 teaspoon vanilla essence

30 g (1 oz) cocoa powder

Beat eggs and sugar in a bowl until light and creamy. Stir through oil, milk and flour.

Divide mixture into two portions. Stir vanilla through one portion and cocoa through the other.

Grease and double line the base of a 6 cup (1.5 litre/48 fl oz) pudding basin. Pour both mixtures into basin and swirl together with a skewer.

Top with a round of greased paper and seal basin with a tight lid or aluminium foil. Place in a large saucepan of simmering water. Cover and cook for 1½ hours or until firm and springy to touch.

**SERVES 6**

# APPLE TOFFEE PUDDING

> 60 g (2 oz) dried apples, chopped
>
> ½ cup (155 ml/5 fl oz) maple syrup
>
> 2 tablespoons hot water
>
> 125 g (4 oz) sugar
>
> 60 g (2 oz) butter
>
> 2 eggs, lightly beaten
>
> 125 g (4 oz) plain flour
>
> 2 teaspoons baking powder
>
> ½ cup (125 ml/4 fl oz) milk
>
> ice cream and maple syrup

Place apples, maple syrup and water in a bowl. Set aside.

Beat sugar and butter in a bowl until light and fluffy. Add eggs, beating well. Fold through sifted flour and baking powder alternately with milk.

Fold apple mixture through. Pour into a greased 6 cup (1.5 litre/48 fl oz) pudding basin. Secure with lid or aluminium foil.

Place in a large saucepan of simmering water. Cover and cook for 1½ hours. Turn pudding onto a serving plate. Serve with ice cream and maple syrup.

**SERVES 6**

# APRICOT CRISP

> 750 g (1½ lb) apricots, halved and stoned
>
> 155 g (5 oz) plain flour
>
> 210 g (7 oz) brown sugar
>
> pinch ground cloves
>
> 1 teaspoon cinnamon
>
> 185 g (6 oz) butter

Preheat oven to 190°C (375°F).

Arrange apricots in greased, shallow ovenproof dish. Mix flour, sugar, cloves and cinnamon and rub in butter until mixture resembles coarse breadcrumbs. Sprinkle mixture evenly over apricots and pack down well. Bake for 30 to 40 minutes until crust is pale brown.

**SERVES 6**

# CHOC CHIP PUDDINGS

> 125 g (4 oz) butter
>
> 250 g (8 oz) sugar
>
> 4 eggs, lightly beaten
>
> 60 g (2 oz) soft fresh breadcrumbs
>
> ½ cup (125 ml/4 fl oz) orange juice
>
> 250 g (8 oz) self-raising flour
>
> 185 g (6 oz) choc chips
>
> Custard (see recipe, page 21)

Beat butter and sugar in a bowl until light and fluffy. Add eggs slowly, beating well.

Fold through breadcrumbs, orange juice, flour and choc bits.

Grease six 1 cup (250 ml/8 fl oz) ramekins or small moulds. Divide mixture between ramekins. Cover with greased paper and aluminium foil. Tie with string to form a tight seal.

Place in a saucepan of simmering water. Cover and cook for 30 minutes. Serve with Custard or cream.

**SERVES 6**

# STICKY DATE PUDDING

**PUDDING**

> 60 g (2 oz) butter
>
> 1 teaspoon almond essence
>
> 250 g (8 oz) sugar
>
> 2 eggs
>
> 90 g (3 oz) self-raising flour
>
> 155 g (5 oz) dates, chopped
>
> 2 cups (500 ml/16 fl oz) water
>
> 1 teaspoon bicarbonate soda

**SAUCE**

> 50 g (1¾ oz) butter
>
> 45 g (1½ oz) brown sugar
>
> ½ cup (125 ml/4 fl oz) cream
>
> 1 tablespoon brandy
>
> cream

Preheat oven to 180°C (350°F).

To Make Pudding: Beat butter, almond essence and sugar in a bowl until light and fluffy. Add eggs, beating well. Fold through flour.

Place dates and water in a saucepan over high heat. Bring to the boil. Boil for 2 minutes. Remove from heat and add bicarbonate.

Fold date mixture through butter mixture. Pour into a greased 18 cm (7 in) square cake tin. Bake for 20 minutes or until cooked when tested with a skewer.

To Make Sauce: Simmer butter, sugar, cream and brandy in a saucepan until reduced by one-third. Pour over pudding. Serve warm with cream.

**SERVES 8**

# Sauces

Master a few of these delicious sauces to turn a simple dessert into a stunning one.
Some of these recipes can be served hot or cold, made ahead of time and stored in the refrigerator.

## CREAMY CARAMEL SAUCE

250 g (8 oz) sugar
½ cup (125 ml/4 fl oz) water
350 ml (12 fl oz) cream

Stir sugar and water in a saucepan over low heat until sugar dissolves.

Bring mixture to the boil. Simmer for 7 minutes or until golden brown.

Very carefully add cream. Stir until smooth. Serve warm or cold.

**MAKES 2 CUPS (500 ML/16 FL OZ)**

## HARD SAUCE

This sauce is great with warm fruit puddings. The sauce melts into the pudding, making it moist and buttery. Use your favourite liqueur that complements your pudding.

85 g (3 oz) butter
250 g (8 oz) icing sugar
1 teaspoon vanilla essence
2 tablespoons liqueur

Beat butter in a bowl until light and fluffy. Gradually beat in icing sugar.

Stir through vanilla and liqueur. Refrigerate for 30 minutes or until firm.

**MAKES 2 CUPS (500 ML/16 FL OZ)**

## CITRUS SAUCE

2 cups (500 ml/16 fl oz) orange juice
3 tablespoons lemon juice
2 tablespoons sugar
3 teaspoons grated lime rind
1 tablespoon cornflour
2 tablespoons brandy

Heat orange and lemon juice, sugar and lime rind in a saucepan until boiling.

Combine cornflour and brandy. Mix to a smooth paste. Add to saucepan. Stir until mixture boils and thickens. Serve hot or cold.

**MAKES 2 CUPS (500 ML/16 FL OZ)**

## CHOCOLATE FUDGE SAUCE

250 g (8 oz) dark chocolate
½ cup (125 ml/4 fl oz) water
30 g (1 oz) butter, chopped
1 tablespoon brandy

In a bowl over a saucepan of simmering water, stir chocolate and water until smooth.

Remove from heat. Stir through butter and brandy. Serve hot or cold. Store in a screw top jar in refrigerator.

**MAKES 1 ½ CUPS (375 ML/12 FL OZ)**

## CREME ANGLAISE

2½ cups (625 ml/20 fl oz) milk
6 egg yolks
125 g (4 oz) sugar
1 teaspoon vanilla essence

In a saucepan, bring milk to the boil. Beat egg yolks and sugar in a bowl until light and fluffy. Pour over boiling milk while still whisking.

Return to saucepan. Stir over low heat until mixture forms a thin custard that coats the back of a spoon. Add vanilla and serve.

**MAKES 3 CUPS (750 ML/24 FL OZ)**

## PRALINE CUSTARD

125 g (4 oz) sugar
¼ cup (60 ml/2 fl oz) water
60 g (2 oz) slivered almonds
1 quantity Custard (see recipe on following page)

Stir sugar and water in a saucepan over low heat until sugar dissolves. Bring to the boil and simmer until golden brown.

Place almonds on a greased baking tray. Pour over toffee. Leave to set before crushing finely.

Stir praline through custard at the end of the cooking time.

**MAKES 2 ½ CUPS (625 ML/20 FL OZ)**

## BERRY SAUCE

*125 g (4 oz) sugar*

*2 cups (500 ml/8 fl oz) water*

*350 g (11 oz) mixed berries*

*2 large pieces lemon peel*

*2 teaspoons cornflour*

Stir sugar and water in a saucepan over low heat until sugar dissolves. Add berries and lemon peel. Simmer for 3 minutes. Remove berries and set aside. Discard peel.

Increase temperature and boil until syrup reduces by one-third. Mix cornflour with a little water and stir into syrup.

Stir until sauce boils and thickens. Return berries to pan. Serve hot or cold.

**MAKES 2 CUPS
(500 ML/16 FL OZ)**

## CUSTARD

*2 teaspoons cornflour*

*2 cups (500 ml/16 fl oz) milk*

*2 egg yolks*

*1 egg*

*2 tablespoons sugar*

*1 teaspoon vanilla essence*

Blend cornflour with a little of the milk in a bowl. Set aside.

Heat remaining milk in a saucepan until almost boiling. Add cornflour mixture and stir until mixture boils and thickens.

Remove from heat and cool slightly. Whisk in egg yolks, egg, sugar and vanilla. Return to low heat and stir for 2 minutes. Serve hot.

**MAKES 2¹/₂ CUPS
(625 ML/20 FL OZ)**

*Sauces from back: Brandy Custard, Chocolate Fudge Sauce, Creamy Caramel Sauce, Berry Sauce*

## BRANDY CUSTARD

*1 quantity of Custard (see recipe above)*

*3 tablespoons brandy*

Make custard according to directions but replace sugar with brown sugar. Stir through brandy at the end of cooking.

**MAKES 2¹/₂ CUPS
(625 ML/20 FL OZ)**

White plates and jug from Waterford Wedgwood,
blue and white plate from Accoutrement

# Family Favourites

**D**ishes that have been star attractions at family gatherings for generations. These classic recipes are scrumptious and dependable.

# Sugar and Spice and All Things Nice

Sugars and spices are features of many sweet temptations. There is a wide variety of commonly used spices available in most local supermarkets but increasingly now we are using more unusual spices and these can be bought in Asian and health food stores. Knowing your ingredients and their qualities will make your shopping and cooking much easier. A few common sugars and spices are detailed here.

## SUGARS

WHITE SUGAR OR GRANULATED SUGAR: The most common medium sized grain sugar used for general table use or cooking.

CASTER SUGAR: This sugar is much finer than granulated sugar and dissolves much faster. Often used in baking meringues or pastries.

BROWN SUGAR: Is a soft moist sugar with a very small crystal.

Each small crystal has a thin film of molasses. This sugar dissolves easily and is often used in fruit cakes and puddings.

RAW SUGAR: Is a large crystal sugar made up of sucrose, ash and water, giving it its characteristic colour. Often thought to be nutritionally superior although this is not true. Used in baking and for decorative purposes.

ICING SUGAR: Is made by grinding selected granulated sugar to a fine powder. Used in baking and desserts as well as for icings and toppings.

DEMERARA SUGAR: Is a raw brown sugar which undergoes a special cleaning process. Has a slightly caramel flavour and is used in baking.

## SPICE

CINNAMON: Can be purchased in quills or bark or in a ground powder form. Must be stored in an airtight container.

CLOVES: Are dried aromatic flower buds from a tree of the myrtle family. Can be used whole

*Pictured on previous pages: Crème Caramel (page 35), Strawberry Shortcake (page 28), Deep Dish Apple Pie (page 30)*

and removed before eating or can be used in a ground powder form.

NUTMEG: Is the dried kernel or nut also from the myrtle family of trees. Can be used whole but is best used freshly grated or ground.

STAR ANISE: Is the dried fruit of a chinese evergreen tree. Tastes of sweet liquorice and can be used both whole and ground.

ALLSPICE: Is the dried unripe fruit of a Jamaican evergreen tree. Tastes like a combination of cinnamon, nutmeg and cloves although it is not. Used whole as a pickling spice and ground as a spice in desserts and baking.

VANILLA: Vanilla pods or beans are the fruits of a vanilla orchid. Vanilla pods are cured to produce their flavour.

# LEMON MERINGUE PIE

A well-loved favourite for all ages. Makes an excellent birthday cake.

## PASTRY

125 g (4 oz) butter

250 g (8 oz) plain flour

90 g (3 oz) caster sugar

1 egg

iced water

## FILLING

3 tablespoons cornflour

125 g (4 oz) sugar

½ cup (125 ml/4 fl oz) lemon juice

1 cup (250 ml/8 fl oz) water

2 egg yolks

3 teaspoons grated lemon rind

30 g (1 oz) butter

## MERINGUE

4 egg whites

90 g (3 oz) sugar

To Make Pastry: Process butter, flour and sugar in a food processor until mixture resembles fine breadcrumbs. Add egg and enough water to form a soft dough. Wrap in plastic wrap and refrigerate for 30 minutes.

Preheat oven to 220°C (425°F).

Roll out dough on a lightly floured surface to fit a 23 cm (9 in) pie dish. Prick sides and base of dough. Bake for 10 minutes or until lightly golden. Set aside.

*Lemon Meringue Pie*

To Make Filling: Mix cornflour, sugar and lemon juice in a saucepan until smooth. Add water. Stir over medium heat until thick. Remove from heat and cool slightly. Whisk through egg yolks, lemon rind and butter. Pour into pastry shell and refrigerate for 1 hour or until firm.

To Make Meringue: Beat egg whites in a bowl until stiff peaks form. Gradually add sugar. Beat until thick and glossy. Pile on top of lemon mixture.

Reduce oven temperature to 160°C (325°F) and bake for 5 minutes or until meringue is light brown.

**SERVES 8**

# CUSTARD TARTS

## PASTRY

125 g (4 oz) butter
125 g (4 oz) sugar
250 g (8 oz) plain flour
iced water

## CUSTARD

3 eggs
2 tablespoons sugar, extra
1½ cups (375 ml/12 fl oz) milk
1 teaspoon vanilla essence
grated nutmeg

To Make Pastry: Process butter, sugar and flour in a food processor until mixture resembles fine breadcrumbs. Add enough water to form a soft dough. Wrap in plastic wrap and refrigerate for 30 minutes.

Preheat oven to 200°C (400°F).

Roll pastry on a lightly floured surface to 5 mm (¼ in) thickness. Cut pastry into four and divide between four small pie tins. Prick the base and sides of pastry with a fork. Bake for 6 minutes or until lightly golden.

To Make Custard: Whisk eggs, sugar, milk and vanilla in bowl to combine. Pour into pastry cases. Sprinkle on nutmeg. Reduce oven temperature to 180°C (350°F). Bake for 25 to 30 minutes or until custard is set.

**SERVES 4**

# RHUBARB CRUMBLE

## CRUMBLE

8 stalks rhubarb, chopped
3 apples, peeled, cored and chopped
½ cup (125 ml/4 fl oz) apricot juice

## TOPPING

185 g (6 oz) muesli
3 tablespoons honey
80 g (2½ oz) butter, melted
½ teaspoon ground cinnamon

Preheat oven to 180°C (350°F).

To Make Crumble: Cook rhubarb, apples and apricot juice in a saucepan over moderate heat for 6 minutes or until soft. Place fruit mixture in a greased ovenproof dish.

To Make Topping: In a bowl, combine muesli, honey, butter and cinnamon. Spoon over fruit. Bake for 15 minutes or until topping is golden and crisp.

**SERVES 6**

*Rhubarb Crumble and Custard Tarts*

# GRANDMA'S CREAMY CHEESECAKE

## BASE

250 g (8 oz) sweet plain biscuits, crushed

125 g (4 oz) butter, melted

## FILLING

250 g (8 oz) cream cheese, softened

250 g (8 oz) ricotta cheese

3 eggs, lightly beaten

185 g (6 oz) caster sugar

2 tablespoons cornflour

1 cup (250 ml/8 fl oz) sour cream

2 tablespoons grated lemon rind

3 tablespoons lemon juice

lemon curd and cream

Preheat oven to 160°C (325°F).

To Make Base: Mix biscuit crumbs and butter in a bowl. Press into a 20 cm (8 in) springform tin and chill until required.

To Make Filling: Process cream cheese and ricotta in a food processor until smooth.

Add eggs, sugar, cornflour, sour cream, lemon rind and juice. Process until smooth.

Pour over refrigerated base. Bake for 50 minutes or until firm. Refrigerate until cold. Serve with lemon curd and cream.

**SERVES 8**

# LEMON CURD

4 lemons

180 g (6 oz) butter or margarine

500 g (1 lb) sugar

4 eggs

Finely grate rind of the lemons. Cut lemons in half. Extract juice and discard pips.

Melt butter and sugar in a bowl set over a pan of hot water. Stir until smooth, without boiling. Blend lemon rind and juice into mixture.

Beat eggs in another bowl. Whisk them into lemon mixture. Place over low heat. Continue to whisk, without boiling until mixture is thick and creamy.

Meanwhile, heat sterilised jars in a low oven. When curd is ready, pour into jars. Cover curd surface with discs of waxed paper.

Cover jars tightly and leave to cool. The curd will set to a jam-like texture. Store in a cool place. Use within one month of making.

**MAKES ABOUT 1 KG (2 LB)**

# PAVLOVA

## BASE

5 egg whites

250 g (8 oz) caster sugar

1 tablespoon cornflour

1 teaspoon vinegar

## TOPPING

1 cup (250 ml/8 fl oz) cream, whipped

sliced fresh fruit

chocolate shavings

Preheat oven to 120°C (250°F).

To Make Base: Place a sheet of non-stick baking paper on a baking tray and mark a 23 cm (9 in) circle.

Beat egg whites in a bowl until stiff peaks form. Gradually add caster sugar and cornflour, beating well after each addition. Fold through vinegar.

Spread or pipe mixture onto marked circle. Bake for 2 hours or until dry and firm.

Decorate with whipped cream, fresh fruit and chocolate shavings.

**SERVES 6**

# STRAWBERRY SHORTCAKE

250 g (8 oz) butter, softened

125 g (4 oz) sugar

1 teaspoon vanilla essence

125 g (4 oz) self-raising flour

45 g (1½ oz) cornflour

155 g (5 oz) plain flour

350 g (11 oz) strawberries, hulled

155 g (5 oz) berry jam, warmed

cream

Preheat oven to 180°C (350°F).

Beat butter, sugar and vanilla in a bowl until light and fluffy. Add flours and mix to form a soft dough.

Knead lightly. Press into a 25 cm (10 in) recessed flan tin.

Bake for 25 minutes or until golden. Cool in tin.

Invert shortcake onto a serving plate. Top with strawberries. Brush well with jam. Serve with cream.

**SERVES 8**

*Pavlova, Grandma's Creamy Cheesecake*

# DEEP DISH APPLE PIE

**PASTRY**

250 g (8 oz) plain flour
125 g (4 oz) butter
1 egg yolk
iced water

**FILLING**

6 apples, peeled and sliced
2 tablespoons sugar
2 tablespoons water
1 clove
½ teaspoon ground cinnamon
milk
extra sugar
cream or ice cream

Preheat oven to 220°C (425°F).

To Make Pastry: Process flour and butter in a food processor until mixture resembles fine breadcrumbs.

Add egg yolk and enough water to form a soft dough. Wrap in plastic wrap. Refrigerate for 30 minutes.

Cut pastry into thirds. Wrap one portion and set aside. Lightly knead the remaining two portions together. Roll out on a lightly floured board to fit the base and up the sides of a deep 23 cm (9 in) springform tin.

To Make Filling: Simmer apples, sugar, water, clove and cinnamon in a saucepan over moderate heat for 8 minutes or until apples are soft. Drain well and remove clove.

Place apples in the tin, stacking them firmly on top of each other.

Roll remaining piece of dough to fit the top of the pie. Seal the edges together with a little milk. Brush the top with milk and sprinkle with extra sugar.

Bake for 15 minutes. Reduce oven temperature to 180°C (350°F). Bake for a further 20 minutes or until pastry is golden. Stand in tin for 5 minutes before serving. Serve with cream or ice cream.

**SERVES 8**

*Deep Dish Apple Pie*

# CHRISTMAS PUDDING

*400 g (13 oz) plain flour*

*450 g (14 oz) shredded suet*

*675 g (1½ lb) currants*

*450 g (14 oz) raisins*

*350 g (11 oz) sultanas*

*100 g (3½ oz) mixed peel*

*50 g (1¾ oz) blanched almonds, chopped*

*100 g (3½ oz) ground almonds*

*225 g (7½ oz) fresh white breadcrumbs*

*450 g (14 oz) soft dark brown sugar*

*2 teaspoons mixed spice*

*4 eggs*

*¼ cup (60 ml/2 fl oz) whisky*

*½ cup (125 ml/4 fl oz) milk*

*finely grated rind 2 lemons and 2 oranges*

*juice 1 lemon and 1 orange*

*few drops each vanilla and almond essence*

*sugar for dredging*

Mix the flour, suet, dried fruits, mixed peel, almonds, breadcrumbs, sugar and spice together.

Beat the eggs with the whisky, milk, lemon and orange rind and juice, and essences.

Stir the two mixtures together very well. Divide the mixture between two well-greased 1 litre (1¾ pint) basins.

Cover with greased greaseproof paper and aluminium foil and secure with string. Cover with a pudding cloth. Put each pudding in a saucepan with boiling water to come halfway up the sides of the basin, cover and steam for 7 to 8 hours, topping up with boiling water.

Allow the cooked puddings to cool. Recover and store in a cool place.

On the day of serving, steam the pudding again for 2 to 3 hours. Turn out and dredge with sugar. Serve very hot with custard, cream or brandy butter.

**MAKES 2 (EACH PUDDING SERVES 6)**

# PEACH BROWN BETTY

*155 g (5 oz) fresh breadcrumbs*

*6 peaches, peeled, pitted and sliced*

*60 g (2 oz) slivered almonds, toasted*

*270 g (9 oz) maple syrup*

*⅓ cup (80 ml/2½ fl oz) water*

*45 g (1½ oz) brown sugar*

*cream or ice cream*

Preheat oven to 160°C (325°F).

Place one-third of the breadcrumbs in the base of a large ovenproof dish.

Top with half the peaches and almonds. Repeat layers and finish with remaining breadcrumbs.

Combine maple syrup, water and brown sugar in a bowl and pour on top of the breadcrumbs.

Bake for 1¼ hours or until golden. Serve with cream or ice cream.

**SERVES 6**

# PEACH AND CHERRY COBBLER

Canned fruit can be substituted for fresh in this recipe.

*4 peaches, peeled and sliced*

*250 g (8 oz) cherries, stems removed and pitted*

*3 tablespoons caster sugar*

*½ cup (125 ml/4 fl oz) water*

**TOPPING**

*90 g (3 oz) self-raising flour*

*2 tablespoons sugar*

*1 teaspoon ground cinnamon*

*60 g (2 oz) butter*

*1 egg, lightly beaten*

*2 tablespoons milk*

Preheat oven to 180°C (350°F).

Simmer peaches, cherries, sugar and water in a saucepan for 8 minutes or until fruit is soft. Pour fruit mixture into a greased, ovenproof dish. Set aside.

To Make Topping: Combine flour, sugar and cinnamon in a bowl. Rub through butter with fingertips. Stir in egg and milk.

Place spoonfuls of mixture around the sides of the dish. Bake for 40 minutes or until top is puffed and golden.

**SERVES 6**

# JAM PUDDING

*3 tablespoons berry jam*

*60 g (2 oz) butter, softened*

*60 g (2 oz) sugar*

*125 g (4 oz) self-raising flour*

*1 egg, lightly beaten*

*3 tablespoons milk*

*½ teaspoon vanilla essence*

*cream or ice cream*

Grease a 6 cup (1.5 litre/48 fl oz) pudding basin. Spread jam across the base.

Beat butter and sugar in a bowl until light and creamy. Fold through flour, egg, milk and vanilla. Pour into pudding basin over jam. Secure pudding with a lid or aluminium foil and string.

Place in a saucepan of boiling water and cook for 1½ hours. Invert onto a serving plate and serve with cream or ice cream.

**SERVES 6**

# Fragrant Flowers

Candied and crystallised flowers, petals and leaves, have been used
for centuries as sweet treats. Exquisitely decorative, they preserve the plant by coating it in sugar
which crystallises with repeated boiling and evaporation.

## CANDIED AND CRYSTALLISED

What is the difference between candied and crystallised fruits and flowers? Very little. Candied fruits are preserved by boiling with sugar until a thick syrup forms. Crystallised fruits are also boiled with sugar and then rolled in extra sugar to coat with crystals. Blossoms or petals are too delicate to be boiled, so the sugar syrup is poured over them and they are left to set.

CANDIED BLOSSOMS: Sweet flowers such as roses, violets, wattle, honeysuckle, sweet peas and scented geraniums, are all edible. They are exquisite when candied and used to decorate a special dessert or cake, and can add that crowning glory to a homemade ice cream or sorbet. Alternatively, you can offer them in a bowl as a sweet.

> *3 cups or handfuls edible blooms (weight depends on choice of flower)*

> *2 cups (500 ml/16 fl oz) water*
> *750 g (24 oz) white sugar*

Wash the flowers briefly and very carefully. Remove stems and gently pat dry. Place water and sugar in a heavy-based saucepan and heat slowly to dissolve sugar. Once sugar has dissolved, bring to the boil and boil until small cracks form, about 138°C (270°F) on a sugar thermometer. Pour about half the syrup into a shallow pan. Let both quantities cool. Position the flowers on a metal rack inside the pan so that they float on the syrup. Cover with a cloth and leave to stand in a cool place for several hours. Spoon over the remaining syrup to completely cover the flowers. Cover again with a cloth and stand for at least 12 hours in a cool place.

Remove the rack and place it on a tray to drain. Store flowers in an airtight container with sheets of baking paper between each flower to prevent them from sticking to each other.

CRYSTALLISED PETALS AND LEAVES: Sugar-coated herb petals and leaves are a beautiful way to preserve herbs. Use to decorate desserts or cakes, or offer as a sweet with coffee.

> *1 cup edible petals or herb leaves (weight depends on flower chosen)*
> *1 egg white*
> *tiny pinch salt*
> *fine vanilla-spiced or caster sugar*

Wash petals or leaves carefully. Pat dry gently with absorbent kitchen paper (do not rinse wattle). Leave flowers whole if very small. Beat egg white with the salt until foamy. Brush it on each petal, flower or leaf with a pastry brush or your fingers. Surfaces should be moist but with no excess egg white.

Shake or dust sugar on both sides. Place gently on a tray lined with baking powder. Dry in the refrigerator for 2 to 3 days. Store in an airtight container in the refrigerator until required.

## GERANIUMS

VARIETIES: Rose geranium
(*Pelargonium graveolens*),
Peppermint geranium
(*Pelargonium tomentosum*),
Coconut geranium
(*Pelargonium enossularoides*),
Lemon geranium
(*Pelargonium limonium*)

PLANT DESCRIPTION:
Geraniums can be planted
anywhere, including rockeries.
They need sun and can withstand
dryness and great heat. Hardy
perennials, all have highly
perfumed leaves with small,
undistinctive flowers that repel
most garden pests. They are all
quick land colonisers and fast
growers.

Rose geranium has a bushy
upright habit and a delicious smell.
Peppermint geranium is low-
growing and trailing. Lemon
geranium grows into a tall bush
and emits a very strong perfume.
Coconut geranium smells, as its
name suggests, of coconut and is
the only scented geranium suitable
for inclusion in a potpourri.

USES: Bruised lemon or rose
geraniums add fragrance to finger
bowls. A leaf or two in milk
puddings, jellies and egg custards
adds a piquant flavour. Try placing
a crushed handful of scented
geranium leaves under the hot tap,
for a fragrant bath.

*Cake beautifully decorated with candied
and crystallised flowers*

## SCENTED SUGAR

Vanilla sugar is well known and
available commercially. It is also
easily made by storing a vanilla
bean in a jar with caster sugar.
What about using scented
geranium leaves for a change?

Scented geraniums are among
the most fragrant plants in the
herb garden. The variety available
includes almond, apple, lemon,
lime, nutmeg, peppermint and
rose geranium. The flavour of
these leaves is easily transferred to
sugar, by simply layering a handful
through a jar of caster sugar. Rose
petals, violets, wattle and mints
will do the same. Leave the leaves,
flowers or petals in the container
of sugar and close tightly for a
couple of weeks. Use to flavour
cakes, biscuits, custards, creams,
sorbets, ice cream or even tea.

Custard is made from a base of milk and egg yolks. It must be cooked gently and stirred frequently to prevent it curdling. Once you have perfected the art of making a good custard you can flavour and sweeten it to taste, use it as a filling for pastries and cakes or simply as an accompaniment to your favourite stewed fruit. These recipes will give you some idea of the many ways you can enhance the simple charm of this underrated dessert. A basic custard recipe is included on page 21.

# BAKED CUSTARD

A recipe to take you back down memory lane to Grandma's place.

*4 eggs, lightly beaten*
*60 g (2 oz) sugar*
*3 cups (750 ml/24 fl oz) milk*
*1 teaspoon vanilla essence*
*125 g (4 oz) sultanas (optional)*
*freshly grated nutmeg*

Preheat oven to 160°C (325°F).

Whisk eggs, sugar, milk and vanilla in a bowl to combine.

Grease a 6 cup (1.5 litre/48 fl oz) ovenproof dish. Sprinkle the base with sultanas and pour over egg mixture. Top with grated nutmeg.

Place in a baking dish half filled with hot water. Bake for 15 to 20 minutes or until set.

**SERVES 4 TO 6**

# PEAR AND ALMOND CUSTARD

*4 pears, peeled, cored and quartered*
*1¼ cups (300 ml/10 fl oz) water*
*150 g (5 oz) caster sugar*
*50g (1¾ oz) blanched almonds*
*few drops almond essence*
*2 egg yolks*
*25 g (1 oz) cornflour*
*1¼ cups (300 ml/10 fl oz) cream*
*4 glacé cherries*
*1 tablespoon flaked almonds*

Place the pears, water and sugar together in a saucepan and bring to the boil. Poach until the pears are tender.

Strain off the syrup and liquidise in a blender with the blanched almonds and almond essence.

Blend the egg yolks, cornflour and 30 ml (1 fl oz) of the cream together in a bowl. Then stir in the syrup and the rest of the cream.

Reheat in a saucepan to boiling point, then allow to cool.

Divide the pears between four attractive glasses and pour in the almond custard.

Decorate with glacé cherries and flaked almonds. Chill before serving.

**SERVES 4**

---

## SEASONAL PEARS

If fresh pears are out of season or unavailable you can always substitute canned pears.

---

# RICE CUSTARD

*4 tablespoons rice*
*4 cups (1 litre/32 fl oz) milk*
*90 g (3 oz) sugar*
*1 tablespoon butter, melted*
*ground cinnamon*

Preheat oven to 140°C (275°F).

Place rice in the base of a greased 6 cup (1.5 litre/48 fl oz) ovenproof dish.

Combine milk, sugar and butter in a bowl. Pour over rice. Sprinkle with cinnamon.

Bake for 1 to 1½ hours or until set and rice is soft.

**SERVES 4 TO 6**

# CREME BRULEE

Choose your favourite stewed fruit to go in the base of the brulées.

*1 cup stewed fruit (weight will vary according to fruit chosen)*
*8 egg yolks*
*3 cups (750 ml/24 fl oz) cream*
*1 vanilla bean*
*brown sugar*

Place fruit in the bottom of six small ramekins. Place egg yolks, cream and vanilla in a saucepan and stir over moderate heat until mixture thickens. Remove vanilla bean. Pour mixture into ramekins. Refrigerate for 6 hours or until set.

Sieve brown sugar over top of custard to form an even coating. Heat under a preheated grill until sugar melts. Serve hot.

**SERVES 6**

# ALMOND COFFEE CREAM

*2 eggs*

*150 g (5 oz) caster sugar*

*1 cup (250 ml/8 fl oz) double cream*

*100 g (3½ oz) almonds*

*¼ cup (60 ml/2 fl oz) cold black coffee*

*100 g (3½ oz) icing sugar*

*24 coffee-flavoured sweets to garnish*

Preheat oven to 200°C (400°F).

Separate the eggs and place the yolks in a bowl. You will not need the whites. Place the bowl containing the egg yolks in a basin of hot, but not boiling, water. Add the sugar to the yolks and whisk the mixture thoroughly for 3 minutes. Gradually pour in 50 ml (2 fl oz) of the cream and continue to whisk until the mixture is thick and smooth.

Place the almonds in a small saucepan with just enough water to cover them. Bring the water to the boil and remove the saucepan from the heat. Drain and refresh the almonds and peel off their skins. Chop them into fine slithers. Wrap them in aluminium foil and place in the preheated oven for 2 minutes. Allow them to cool in the foil.

Reserve 15 g (½ oz) of the almond slithers and mix the rest into the egg mixture.

Whip the remaining cream and stir in the black coffee. Gently fold in the icing sugar. Mix this coffee cream with the egg yolk mixture. Pour the cream into 4 individual serving dishes. Place them in the refrigerator to chill for at least 4 hours. Sprinkle with the reserved almonds, garnish with the coffee-flavoured sweets and serve.

**SERVES 4**

**BLANCHING ALMONDS**

To blanch almonds, just pour boiling water over them and leave for a few minutes. Remove the skins by squeezing the end of each nut — the almond will then pop out!

# CREME CARAMEL

**CARAMEL**

*250 g (8 oz) sugar*

*½ cup (125 ml/4 fl oz) water*

**CUSTARD**

*300 ml (10 fl oz) cream*

*1½ cups (375 ml/12 fl oz) milk*

*1 vanilla bean*

*4 eggs*

*80 g (2½ oz) sugar*

*cream*

Preheat oven to 160°C (325°F).

To Make Caramel: Stir sugar and water in a saucepan over low heat until sugar dissolves. Bring to the boil and simmer for 6 minutes or until a light golden. Pour caramel into the bases of six greased moulds. Set aside.

To Make Custard: Heat cream, milk and vanilla bean in a saucepan until boiling. Remove from heat. Discard vanilla bean. In a bowl beat eggs and sugar until light and fluffy. Pour over hot milk mixture, while beating.

Pour mixture into moulds. Set in a baking tray half filled with water. Bake for 35 to 45 minutes or until set. Refrigerate until cold. Invert onto serving plates and serve with cream.

**SERVES 6**

# GRANDMOTHER'S SHORTCAKE

*1 quantity short pastry (see Cherry Shortcake recipe on page 38)*

*300 g (10 oz) ricotta*

*100 g (3½ oz) amaretti or macaroon biscuits, crushed*

*70 g (2⅓ oz) butter*

*50 g (1¾ oz) raisins*

*50 g (1¾ oz) bitter chocolate, grated*

*2 egg yolks*

*2 tablespoons Amaretto liqueur or rum*

Line a baking dish with the pastry. In a bowl, cream the ricotta with the sugar, add the crushed biscuits, liqueur, raisins, chocolate and egg yolks. Fill the lined baking dish with this mixture, decorate with pastry ribbons and bake for 45 minutes. Serve cold.

**SERVES 6**

# PECAN PIE

## PASTRY

125 g (4 oz) plain flour
1 tablespoon caster sugar
1 tablespoon custard powder
90 g (3 oz) butter
iced water

## FILLING

250 g (8 oz) sugar
270 g (9 oz) golden syrup
45 g (1½ oz) butter, melted
165 g (5½ oz) pecan nuts
3 eggs, lightly beaten

To Make Pastry: Process flour, sugar, custard powder and butter in a food processor until mixture resembles fine breadcrumbs.

Add enough iced water to form a soft dough. Wrap in plastic and refrigerate for 30 minutes.

Preheat oven to 200°C (400°F).

Roll out dough on a lightly floured surface to fit a 23 cm (9 in) loose springform tin. Prick base and sides with a fork. Bake for 10 minutes or until golden.

To Make Filling: Mix sugar, golden syrup and butter in a bowl. Add pecan nuts and eggs. Pour into pastry shell.

Reduce oven temperature to 160°C (325°F) and bake for 50 minutes or until a rich brown colour. Serve sliced, with cream.

**SERVES 8**

# PROFITEROLES WITH CHOCOLATE

## FILLING

1 cup (250 ml/8 fl oz) cream, whipped
1 tablespoon icing sugar
2 tablespoons favourite liqueur
200 g (6½ oz) chocolate, melted

## CHOUX PASTRY

1 cup (250 ml/8 fl oz) water
85 g (3 oz) butter
125 g (4 oz) plain flour
4 eggs, lightly beaten

Preheat oven to 200°C (400°F).

To Make Choux Pastry: Stir water and butter in a saucepan over moderate heat until butter melts. Stir in flour. Continue cooking and stirring until mixture forms a smooth ball.

Place mixture in a bowl and beat, while slowly adding eggs. Beat until mixture is thick and glossy.

Place spoonfuls of mixture onto greased baking trays. Bake for 10 minutes. Reduce temperature to 180°C (350°F) and cook for a further 10 minutes. Pierce bases to allow steam to escape and cool on wire racks.

To Make Filling: Combine cream, icing sugar and liqueur in a bowl. Transfer to a piping bag. Pipe cream into choux puffs from the base.

Dip tops in melted chocolate. Store in refrigerator until ready to serve.

**SERVES 8**

*Profiteroles with Chocolate and Pecan Pie*

## BREAD AND BUTTER PUDDING

*8 slices bread, crusts removed*

*60 g (2 oz) butter, softened*

*125 g (4 oz) sultanas*

*6 eggs*

*185 g (6 oz) caster sugar*

*300 ml (10 fl oz) cream*

*300 ml (10 fl oz) milk*

*1 teaspoon vanilla essence*

*brown sugar*

Preheat oven to 180°C (350°F).

Spread bread with butter and cut into three strips. Place half the bread, butter side up, in a greased 25 cm (10 in) cake tin.

Sprinkle bread with half the sultanas. Top with bread and remaining sultanas.

Whisk together eggs, sugar, cream, milk and vanilla in a bowl until light and fluffy. Pour over bread. Sprinkle with brown sugar and stand for 5 minutes. Bake for 1 hour or until set.

**SERVES 8**

## CHERRY SHORTCAKE

**PASTRY**

*300 g (10 oz) plain flour*

*150 g (5 oz) butter, cut into pieces*

*150 g (5 oz) sugar*

*grated peel of 1 lemon*

*2 eggs*

*pinch of salt*

**FILLING**

*800 g (26 oz) dark red cherries, stoned*

*1 small jar cherry jam*

*2 tablespoons icing sugar*

To Make Pastry: Sift flour onto a board, add salt, sugar and the grated lemon peel, mix together and make a well in the centre. Break in 1 egg and add the butter. Knead with the fingertips, taking care not to work the pastry too much. When smooth, shape into a ball, roll in buttered greaseproof paper and refrigerate for 30 minutes.

Preheat oven to 180°C (350°F).

Roll the pastry out to a thickness of 5 mm (¼ in) and line a buttered and floured tart or quiche dish. Using a pastry wheel, cut the leftover pastry into long ribbons.

Spread the cherry jam on the bottom of the pastry and cover with the washed and stoned cherries. Decorate with the pastry ribbons in a lattice pattern.

Brush the pastry with beaten egg. Bake for 45 minutes.

When cooked, sprinkle with icing sugar.

Serve hot or cold.

**SERVES 6**

## CARAMEL BAKED BANANAS

*4 bananas, sliced lengthways*

*½ teaspoon ground cinnamon*

*2 tablespoons brandy*

*1 cup (250 ml/8 fl oz) sweetened condensed milk*

*ice cream*

Preheat oven to 150°C (300°F).

Place bananas in the bottom of an ovenproof dish. Sprinkle with cinnamon and brandy.

Pour condensed milk evenly over bananas. Place in a baking dish half filled with hot water.

Bake for 45 minutes or until golden brown. Serve with ice cream.

**SERVES 6**

## CHOCOLATE MOUSSE

*350 g (11 oz) dark chocolate, chopped*

*3 eggs, separated*

*1 cup (250 ml/8 fl oz) cream, whipped*

*2 tablespoons brandy or liqueur of your choice*

*berries and chocolate curls*

Stir chocolate in the top of a double boiler over low heat until melted. Remove from heat and cool. Stir egg yolks through chocolate. Fold in cream.

Beat egg whites until soft peaks form. Fold through chocolate with brandy.

Spoon mixture into six individual serving dishes. Refrigerate for 2 hours or until set. Decorate with berries and chocolate curls.

**SERVES 6**

# MANGO LIME TRIFLE

## CUSTARD

3 tablespoons custard powder

1 cup (250 ml/8 fl oz) milk

2 tablespoons lime juice

½ cup (125 ml/4 fl oz) cream, whipped

## FILLING

1 x 85 g (3 oz) packet lemon jelly crystals

1½ cups (375 ml/12 fl oz) boiling water

1 x 20 cm (8 in) sponge cake, sliced

½ cup (125 ml/4 fl oz) rum

3 mangoes, peeled and chopped

1 tablespoon grated lime rind

¾ cup (180 ml/6 fl oz) cream, whipped, extra

To Make Custard: Mix the custard powder with a little of the milk to form a smooth paste. Heat remaining milk in a saucepan. Add custard paste to milk. Stir until custard boils and thickens. Cool then stir through lime juice and cream.

To Make Filling: Place jelly crystals in a lamington tin. Pour over boiling water. Stir until crystals dissolve. Refrigerate until set. Cut into squares.

To Assemble: Place a layer of sponge cake in the base of a glass serving dish. Top with half the rum, custard, mango, lime rind and jelly. Repeat layers and top with extra cream. Chill and allow flavours to develop before serving.

**SERVES 6 TO 8**

# TANGY IMPOSSIBLE PIE

4 eggs, lightly beaten

60 g (2 oz) plain flour

250 g (8 oz) sugar

60 g (2 oz) butter, melted

90 g (3 oz) desiccated coconut, toasted

1 tablespoon grated lemon rind

2 teaspoons grated lime rind

1 tablespoon grated orange rind

½ cup (125 ml/4 fl oz) lime or lemon juice

½ cup (125 ml/4 fl oz) orange juice

½ cup (125 ml/4 fl oz) milk

½ cup (125 ml/4 fl oz) cream

cream or ice cream

Preheat oven to 180°C (350°F).

Process eggs, flour, sugar, butter, coconut, grated rinds, juices, milk and cream in a food processor until smooth.

Pour into a greased, large, rectangular, ovenproof dish. Bake for 1 hour or until golden. Serve warm with cream or ice cream.

**SERVES 6**

---

### ZEST

The outer layer of citrus fruit skin is known as zest. It may be removed by using a grater (ensure only the colour of the skin is removed, as the white pith underneath is bitter) or may be peeled off using a vegetable peeler. These pieces of skin may be sliced thinly, blanched and used in recipes. A zester will make even finer strips, and this peel does not require blanching.

---

# PANCAKES

125 g (4 oz) self-raising flour

2 tablespoons caster sugar

1 egg, lightly beaten

1¼ cups (310 ml/10½ fl oz) milk

Place flour and sugar in a bowl. Make a well in the centre. Mix together egg and milk.

Pour milk mixture into flour. Whisk until smooth.

Pour 3 tablespoons of mixture into a greased frypan. Cook over moderate heat for 1 minute or until large bubbles appear.

Turn pancake and cook other side until golden. Repeat with remaining mixture.

Try these toppings:

• slices of banana and caramel sauce

• maple syrup and whipped butter

• jam and cream

• passionfruit and cream

• ice cream, topping of your choice and crushed nuts

**SERVES 6**

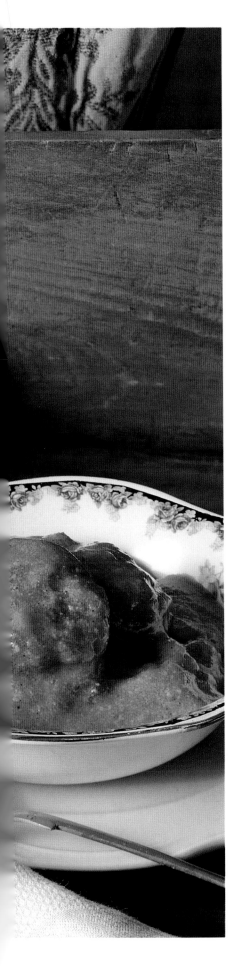

# CINNAMON DUMPLINGS WITH TOFFEE SAUCE

### DUMPLINGS

30 g (1 oz) butter
155 g (5 oz) self-raising flour
125 g (4 oz) golden syrup
⅓ cup (80 ml/2½ fl oz) milk
2 teaspoons ground cinnamon

### TOFFEE SAUCE

60 g (2 oz) butter
200 g (6½ oz) brown sugar
2 cups (500 ml/16 fl oz) milk

To Make Dumplings: Rub butter through flour. Add golden syrup, milk and cinnamon. Mix to a smooth dough. Shape tablespoons of mixture into balls. Set aside.

To Make Toffee Sauce: Stir butter and sugar in a saucepan over low heat until sugar dissolves. Add milk and bring to the boil.

Add dumplings. Simmer, covered, for 25 minutes or until cooked through. Serve in individual bowls with Toffee Sauce.

**SERVES 6**

# LIME AND COCONUT DELICIOUS

3 eggs, separated
125 g (4 oz) sugar
30 g (1 oz) butter, melted
1¼ cups (310 ml/10½ fl oz) milk
2 teaspoons lime rind
⅓ cup (80 ml/2½ fl oz) lime juice
45 g (1½ oz) desiccated coconut
60 g (2 oz) self-raising flour
125 g (4 oz) caster sugar

Preheat oven to 180°C (350°F).

Beat egg yolks and sugar in a bowl until thick and creamy. Fold through butter, milk, lime rind and juice, coconut and flour.

Beat egg whites in another bowl until stiff peaks form. Gradually add sugar, beating until glossy. Fold through lime mixture.

Pour into a greased ovenproof dish. Place in a baking dish half filled with hot water. Bake for 50 minutes or until firm on top but saucy on the base.

**SERVES 6**

*Lime and Coconut Delicious and Cinnamon Dumplings with Toffee Sauce*

# Freezing Desserts

*Y*ou can realise the full potential of your freezer by using it for storing desserts, puddings and cakes. Not only does it make sense to cook in bulk then stow, say, half a dozen of your favourite cheesecakes or apple pies, it also enables you to produce a mouth-watering but impressive sweet at the drop of a hat.

## FREEZING HINTS

If faced with the prospect of unexpected guests or in need of a dependable family favourite, it's then merely a matter of thawing one of your ready-made puds while your hands are free to prepare other courses.

Easiest options are, of course, those delicious home-made ice creams and meringues which require little or no thawing. They can be transformed into an exotic finale to any meal with the simple addition of fresh fruit, a little imaginative decoration or some piped cream.

## GELATINE-BASED DESSERTS

Souffles, chiffons and chilled cheesecakes need more cautious handling. A fairly high proportion of gelatine in the recipe means it's unlikely to freeze successfully, but you can gauge this with a little experimentation. Just save a slice of favourite cheesecake or souffle from one you're serving up and pop it in the freezer for a couple

of weeks. If, after this time, it shrinks or takes on a leathery appearance you'll know it's not an exercise to repeat.

Cooked cheesecakes, on the other hand, fare much better in the freezer. To preserve their appearance they can be frozen in their baking dish, but removed from this once solid and re-wrapped for longer-term storage. That frees your dish for repeated use.

## HOME-MADE PIES AND PUDDINGS

There's nothing like a home-made pie to make the mouth water, but every cook knows they're not turned out in a moment, so it makes sense to cook in bulk and keep a stock in the freezer. Pastry undoubtedly freezes better when uncooked and the pie should ideally be allowed one hour to thaw. If you're in too much of a rush to thaw, remember to give your pie a few extra minutes in the oven — the timespan depends on its size.

Many of the traditional-style 'heavy' desserts like rice, sago and tapioca will freeze well, though they may thin down a little in the process. Steamed puddings should be removed from the steamer as soon as they're cooked, then chilled rapidly, wrapped and frozen, while accompanying sauces should be thickened after thawing.

## PANCAKES

Pancakes are extremely versatile, for both sweet and savoury recipes, but it's important to recognise which types will freeze most effectively. Thin French-style crepes made with eggs will keep very well at icy temperatures, but thick pancakes and those containing little or no egg lose pliability, become tough and will crack. For best results you should place freezer sheeting between each crepe and pack a stack of them in well-sealed freezer bags. Remove as much air as possible from the bag before sealing. Thaw the crepes at room temperature before filling them.

# CAKES

Few people have time these days for the weekly cake-baking session undertaken by our mothers and grandmothers, but with the traditional sponge still a firm family favourite, the answer is simple — keep a frozen cake store.

An unfilled sponge cake will keep successfully for up to four months in a sealed freezer bag with as much air as possible removed beforehand.

The trick in freezing all cakes is to chill them unwrapped until firm, then put them in airtight containers. Filled sponges will keep up to a month in a lidded container and may be sliced into servings before freezing to speed up the thawing process and save you having to defrost an entire cake when just a couple of slices are needed.

Freezer storage space is often at a premium so a handy tip to remember is to save decoration of cakes and desserts until they're thawed. If you don't, you'll find that valuable space is taken up by bulky containers protecting your handiwork, or alternatively you'll be unable to stack other dishes on top of frail confections.

# FRUITFUL FREEZING

With so many delicious fruits enjoying a very short season, it makes sound economic sense to buy them when they're available at low cost and store them in the freezer. However, use the wrong chilling technique and all your cost cutting methods could go to waste. There are three fool-proof methods of storing fruit. Firstly, you can preserve fruits in a syrup pack, with one of three strengths. For a thin syrup, use one cup of sugar to three cups of water; for a medium syrup add one cup of sugar to two cups of water and a thick syrup is made from equal proportions of sugar and water. Then it's simply a matter of boiling the water until the sugar is completely dissolved, and allowing the solution to cool. It should then be gently poured over fruit, packed into a rigid container, just 2 cm (¾ in) short of the top. The syrup should cover the fruit completely, but not entirely fill the container, as liquid expands when frozen.

The second method of storage is dry sugar packing, which involves dipping the fruit into a protective mixture made of the juice of one lemon and two cups of water. Fruit should be dipped once, then sprinkled with sugar and placed in a sealed, airtight freezer bag. This method is, however, only suitable for fruits that will not discolour.

As many of us prefer to keep our fruit sugar-free, the third method of storage (an unsugared or artificially sweetened solution) is a good alternative.

You simply place a freezer bag in a rigid container, then half-fill it with fruit which has been dipped in the protective solution (made from the juice of one lemon and two cups of water). The fruit should then be covered with an unsugared pack solution (one tablespoon of ascorbic acid per 5 cups of water) which may be artificially sweetened if you prefer. Squeeze as much air as possible from the bag, then seal it, and put a lid on the container.

As a rule of thumb, remember that any fruits you find in cans can generally be frozen successfully. However, don't overstretch yourself when embarking on a fruit-freezing operation — prepare too many fruits like peaches, nectarines and pears in one go and you'll find they discolour before you can complete the job. Also, many fruits do not need extensive preparation before freezing — all berry fruits, cherries and rhubarb, for instance, can be free frozen until solid then vacuum packed for longer term and space-saving storage.

Just one final word — before putting any of your frozen fruit packs into the freezer, do take the trouble to label them with the date and details of the contents — it will save much confusion when the time comes to thaw and use them!

Plates from Waterford Wedgwood, fabric from I Redelman and Son

# Fruity and Frothy

*B*ubbly and bouncy
— these recipes
will give a lift to any
meal.

Fruits of all kinds and
from all seasons are
used in these recipes.
There are also recipes
for wonderfully light
soufflés.

Delight your guests
with fresh fruits,
brilliantly presented by
following these lovely
recipes.

# Fruit For All Seasons

*F*ollow these tips for successful purchasing and storage of fresh fruits. Always buy fruit that is in season. It has a far better taste and is much less expensive than fruit that is just coming into or out of season. Select fruit that is free from blemishes or bruising.

## KEEPING THEM CRISP

- For longer life store fruit in the crisper section of your refrigerator. The only exception to this is bananas which need to be stored in a cool dry place.
- Store cut fruit covered with plastic wrap or in airtight containers in the refrigerator. This helps them not to dry out or take on any other smells or odours in the fridge.

## FRUIT FAMILY AND FRIENDS

If a fresh fruit is not available for a recipe you have chosen you may be able to substitute it for another fruit of the same family. This is also a great idea for giving your favourite recipe a new twist. The following groups of fruit all substitute well for each other:

- Apples, pears and nashi pears;
- Oranges, tangelos, mandarins and tangerines;
- Lemons, limes and grapefruit;
- Peaches, nectarines, plums, apricots, mangoes;
- Strawberries, raspberries, blueberries, mulberries, boysenberries and blackberries;
- Watermelon, honeydew, rockmelon or cantaloupe and champagne melons.

## TRUSTY STANDBYS

If fresh fruit is unavailable it may be substituted with dried, canned or frozen fruit. There are only a few rules to remember when substituting to ensure a perfect success.

- Canned fruit must equal the weight of fresh fruit after it has been well drained, not before draining.
- Allow frozen fruit to thaw and drain before weighing.
- Canned fruits often need less cooking time than fresh.
- If substituting dried fruits for fresh, remember to reconstitute them in water before weighing or using.

If you would like to freeze your own fruits, turn to Fruitful Freezing on page 43 for hints on achieving a great result.

*Pictured on previous pages: Poached Tamarillos with Lime Baked Custards (page 64), Cappucino Soufflés (page 47)*

# LAYERED FIG AND MASCARPONE MERINGUE

### MERINGUE

*3 egg whites*

*185 g (6 oz) caster sugar*

*125 g (4 oz) toasted hazelnuts, ground*

### FILLING

*1 cup (250 ml/8 fl oz) cream*

*125 g (4 oz) mascarpone cheese*

*2 tablespoons Irish cream liqueur*

*2 tablespoons icing sugar*

*6 figs, sliced*

### TOPPING

*60 g (2 oz) flaked almonds, toasted*

*icing sugar*

Preheat oven to 140°C (275°F).

Trace twelve 10 cm (4 in) circles onto baking paper and arrange on an oven tray.

To Make Meringues: Beat egg whites in a bowl until soft peaks form. Gradually add sugar, beating until thick and glossy. Fold hazelnuts through meringue.

Spoon mixture into a piping bag fitted with a plain nozzle. Pipe meringue into circles. Bake for 1 hour or until dry and firm.

To Make Filling: Beat cream, mascarpone, liqueur and icing sugar in a bowl until thick.

To Assemble: Spread eight meringue rounds with filling. Top with slices of fig. Sandwich together to make four. Top each with a plain meringue round. Sprinkle with almonds and icing sugar.

**SERVES 4**

# APPLE AND PASSIONFRUIT CRUMBLE

*3 apples, peeled, cored and sliced*

*3 pears, peeled, cored and sliced*

*4 passionfruit*

*2 tablespoons brown sugar*

*½ teaspoon ground cinnamon*

### TOPPING

*155 g (5 oz) rolled oats*

*15 g (½ oz) shredded coconut*

*60 g (2 oz) melted butter*

*2 tablespoons honey*

Preheat oven to 180°C (350°F).

Combine apples, pears, passionfruit, sugar and cinnamon in a bowl. Transfer to an ovenproof dish.

To Make Topping: Mix oats, coconut, butter and honey in a bowl.

Spread topping over apple mixture. Bake for 20 to 30 minutes or until apple is soft and topping is golden.

**SERVES 6 TO 8**

# MANGO AND COCONUT MOUSSE

*2 mangoes, peeled and chopped or 2 x 440 g (14 oz) cans, drained*

*2 tablespoons sugar*

*1 tablespoon grated orange rind*

*1 tablespoon gelatine*

*3 tablespoons boiling water*

*150 ml (5 fl oz) cream*

*150 ml (5 fl oz) coconut cream*

*toasted coconut*

*extra cream*

Puree mangoes in a bowl until smooth. Add sugar and orange rind. Dissolve gelatine in boiling water in a small bowl. Stir into mango puree.

Beat together cream and coconut cream until thick. Fold through mango. Pour into six individual serving dishes. Chill for 4 hours or until set.

Serve with toasted coconut and extra cream.

**SERVES 6**

# CAPPUCCINO SOUFFLES

*3 egg yolks*

*⅓ cup (90 g/3 oz) caster sugar*

*½ cup (125 ml/4 fl oz) milk*

*½ cup (125 ml/4 fl oz) strong black coffee*

*3 teaspoons gelatine*

*3 tablespoons boiling water*

*300 ml (10 fl oz) thickened cream, whipped*

*drinking chocolate powder*

Beat egg yolks and sugar in a bowl until thick and fluffy. Heat milk and coffee in a pan until almost boiling. Pour over egg mixture while continuing to beat. Return mixture to pan and stir over moderate heat until slightly thickened. Cool.

Sprinkle gelatine over boiling water in a small bowl. Stir to dissolve. Fold gelatine and cream through coffee mixture.

Make a 5 cm (2 in) high foil collar around four ½ cup (125 ml/4 fl oz) capacity ramekins. Secure with string. Brush ramekins lightly with oil.

Pour mixture into ramekins and refrigerate for 4 hours or until firm. Remove collars before serving and sprinkle with drinking chocolate.

**SERVES 4**

# SUGAR GRILLED PEARS WITH BRANDY CREAM

6 small pears, peeled, halved and cored

1 cinnamon stick

180 g (6 oz) sugar

## BRANDY CREAM

½ cup (125 ml/4 fl oz) sour cream

½ cup (125 ml/4 fl oz) cream, whipped

1 tablespoon brown sugar

2 to 3 tablespoons brandy

To Prepare Pears: Simmer them in a large saucepan with cinnamon, sugar and water to cover for 6 minutes or until soft. Remove from pan.

Cut pear halves into strips without cutting through top end. Fan out pears on baking trays.

Sprinkle with a little extra sugar. Place under a preheated grill until golden brown.

To Make Brandy Cream: Beat sour cream, cream, sugar and brandy in a bowl until thick. Serve beside pears.

**SERVES 6**

# BANANA TARTINE

## PASTRY

155 g (5 oz) plain flour

155 g (5 oz) butter

30 g (1 oz) ground almonds

2 tablespoons sugar

1 egg yolk

2 tablespoons cold water

## TOPPING

250 g (8 oz) butter

125 g (4 oz) brown sugar

8 firm bananas, halved lengthways

60 g (2 oz) unsalted cashew nuts

Preheat oven to 200°C (400°F).

Process flour and butter in a food processor until mixture resembles fine breadcrumbs. Add almonds, sugar, egg yolk and enough water to form a soft dough. Cover dough and refrigerate for 30 minutes.

To Make Topping: In a large frypan, melt butter over medium heat. Add brown sugar and cook, stirring, for 3 minutes. Add bananas to pan. Cook for 1 minute each side. Carefully transfer bananas and syrup into a 20 cm (8 in) square tin. Sprinkle with cashews.

Roll out pastry to fit tin. Place pastry over bananas. Make three slits for steam to escape. Bake for 30 minutes. Cool in tin for 5 minutes before inverting onto a serving plate.

**SERVES 8**

*Sugar Grilled Pears with Brandy Cream and Banana Tartine*

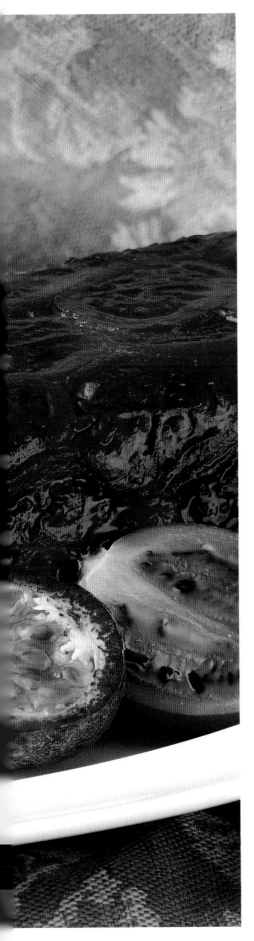

## PASSIONFRUIT AND TAMARILLO TERRINE

8 tamarillos

125 g (4 oz) sugar

4 cups (1 litre/32 fl oz) water

extra tamarillo slices

### PASSIONFRUIT CREAM

6 passionfruit

2 tablespoons sugar

1 tablespoon grated orange rind

2 tablespoons gelatine

⅓ cup (80 ml/2½ fl oz) boiling water

2½ cups (625 ml/20 fl oz) cream, whipped

To Prepare Tamarillos: Place them in a large saucepan of boiling water for 3 minutes. Remove from pan and peel away skins.

Stir sugar and water in a saucepan over low heat until sugar dissolves. Add tamarillos and simmer for 5 minutes or until tamarillos are soft. Cool and slice into rounds.

To Make Passionfruit Cream: Scoop passionfruit into a bowl. Add sugar and orange rind. Dissolve gelatine in boiling water in a small bowl. Cool and stir into passionfruit. Fold passionfruit through whipped cream.

Oil a 9 x 23 cm (3½ x 9 in) terrine dish. Cover base and sides with slices of tamarillo. Reserve some tamarillo for garnish.

Carefully pour in Passionfruit Cream. Cover and refrigerate for 6 hours or until set. Invert terrine onto a serving plate. Serve sliced, with extra tamarillo slices.

**SERVES 6 TO 8**

*Passionfruit and Tamarillo Terrine*

## MELON PARFAIT

½ yellow champagne melon

¼ watermelon

½ rockmelon

½ honeydew melon

extra nuts

### MACADAMIA CREAM

60 g (2 oz) macadamia nuts, lightly toasted

2 tablespoons honey

2 cups (500 ml/16 fl oz) cream, whipped

Cut all the melons into balls or small cubes. Refrigerate until required.

To Make Macadamia Cream: Roughly chop nuts. Combine in a bowl with honey and cream.

Place a layer of melon in the base of six parfait glasses. Spoon over Macadamia Cream and repeat layers until glasses are full. Chill until required. Serve topped with extra nuts.

**SERVES 6**

---

**MELONS**

Melons are delicious in summer. They are 95 percent water so they are a great thirst quencher. Choose fruit that is firm and ripe. A perfect melon has a wonderful aroma. To maintain their freshness, store melons in the refrigerator. Melon looks fabulous served straight from the fruit. Cut your melon in half and remove as much flesh as possible with a melon baller, being careful not to pierce the skin. Make a salad of different varieties of melon and serve them in the hollowed out shells. You can also cut melon in a wide variety of shapes. Try using a small biscuit cutter or a knife.

---

# RHUBARB SOUFFLES

*caster sugar*

*8 stalks rhubarb, cut into 2 cm (¾ in) pieces*

*1 tablespoon grated orange rind*

*½ cup (125 ml/4 fl oz) orange juice*

*½ cup (125 ml/4 fl oz) water*

*1 tablespoon cornflour*

*2 tablespoons brown sugar*

*2 eggs, separated*

*2 egg whites*

Preheat oven to 200°C (400°F).

Grease six 1 cup (250 ml/8 fl oz) ramekins and sprinkle with caster sugar.

Simmer rhubarb, orange rind, juice and water in a saucepan over medium heat for 15 minutes or until rhubarb is very soft.

Rub rhubarb mixture through a sieve. Mix cornflour, brown sugar and egg yolks in a small bowl until smooth. Stir into rhubarb mixture. Return rhubarb mixture to heat. Stir until mixture boils and thickens. Cool slightly.

Beat all egg whites until stiff peaks form. Fold into rhubarb mixture. Spoon into ramekins. Bake for 30 minutes or until puffed and lightly golden.

**SERVES 6**

# CHOCOLATE CHESTNUT BAVAROIS

*8 egg yolks*

*250 g (8 oz) sugar*

*2 cups (500 ml/16 fl oz) milk*

*2 tablespoons cocoa powder*

*2 tablespoons gelatine*

*½ cup (125 ml/4 fl oz) boiling water*

*125 g (4 oz) chestnut puree*

*2½ cups (600 ml/20 fl oz) cream, whipped*

*extra cream and berries*

Grease six 1 cup (250 ml/8 fl oz) bavarois moulds with oil.

Beat egg yolks and sugar in a bowl until thick and fluffy. Heat milk in a pan until almost boiling. Cool to lukewarm.

Stir milk and cocoa into egg yolk mixture. Place over a saucepan of simmering water. Stir until custard is thick enough to coat the back of a spoon.

Dissolve gelatine in boiling water in a small bowl. Add to custard. Add a few tablespoons of custard to chestnut puree and beat until smooth.

Fold chestnut mixture through custard. Cool to lukewarm. Fold through cream.

Divide mixture between moulds. Chill for 4 hours or until set. Unmould and serve with extra cream and berries.

**SERVES 6**

*Chocolate Chestnut Bavarois*

# PEAR DUMPLINGS WITH RHUBARB SAUCE

### DUMPLINGS

*250 g (8 oz) cream cheese*

*125 g (4 oz) plain flour*

*50 g (1¾ oz) butter*

*1 egg*

*1 pear, peeled and chopped into 8 pieces*

*150 g (5 oz) butter, extra*

*200 g (6½ oz) fresh breadcrumbs*

*100 g (3½ oz) sugar*

### RHUBARB SAUCE

*8 stalks rhubarb*

*2 tablespoons sugar, extra*

To Make Dumplings: Combine cream cheese, flour, butter and egg in a bowl. Roll into a sausage shape. Cut into eight equal portions.

Flatten each piece to be large enough to encase a piece of pear. Encase pear and make sure there are no holes. Poach in boiling water for 10 minutes. Drain on absorbent paper.

Melt extra butter in a frypan. Add breadcrumbs and sugar. Stir over heat until golden. Toss dumplings in breadcrumb mixture.

To Make Rhubarb Sauce: In a saucepan cook rhubarb and sugar with a little water until soft. Rub through a sieve and serve with dumplings.

**SERVES 4**

*Pear Dumplings with Rhubarb Sauce*

# BAKED QUINCES IN PASSIONFRUIT CREAM

*4 quinces, peeled, cored and halved*

### PASSIONFRUIT CREAM

*3 to 4 passionfruit*

*125 g (4 oz) sugar*

*1 cup (250 ml/8 fl oz) sour cream*

*1½ cups (375 ml/12 fl oz) cream*

*2 tablespoons cornflour*

Preheat oven to 180°C (350°F).

To Make Passionfruit Cream: Combine passionfruit pulp, sugar, sour cream, cream and cornflour in a bowl and mix well.

Arrange quinces in a large greased ovenproof dish. Pour over passionfruit cream. Cover and bake for 1 hour. Serve warm.

**SERVES 6**

### QUINCES

Quinces are one of the earliest known fruits and originated in Asia. They are similar in texture to apples and pears.
A golden-coloured skin, usually covered in a soft down, encircles the fruit. The flesh is pale when raw, but turns a delightful pink when cooked — the longer they are cooked, the deeper the pink colour will become.
Quinces are a fruit that should be cooked to be enjoyed. They can be stewed in water and sugar until soft. Once stewed they can be used in tarts. Another method is to dry bake them in a moderate oven. When soft, cut them open, remove the core and sprinkle with cinnamon. Serve with cream or natural yoghurt.

## BAKED TANGELOS

*4 tangelos, peeled*

*90 g (3 oz) demerara sugar*

### TOPPING

*4 egg yolks*

*90 g (3 oz) sugar*

*¼ cup (60 ml/2 fl oz) marsala*

*1 tablespoon icing sugar*

Preheat oven to 180°C (350°F).

To Prepare Tangelos: Peel and remove any pith from tangelos. Arrange in a large, greased, ovenproof dish.

Sprinkle with sugar. Bake for 12 minutes or until soft.

To Make Topping: Place egg yolks and sugar in a bowl over a saucepan of simmering water. Beat with an electric mixer until mixture is very thick. Beat in marsala.

Pour mixture over tangelos. Sprinkle with icing sugar. Place under a preheated grill for 4 minutes or until top is lightly browned. Serve immediately.

**SERVES 6**

---

### TANGELOS

A tangelo is a cross between a mandarin and a grapefruit. They are larger than the average mandarin and are very juicy. Easily broken into segments, tangelos are great in salads and fruit platters.

---

### FRUIT TARTS

Try adding citrus juice to the filling for added zest. Make your tart shine by warming some jam and brushing it over the arranged fruit.

---

## FRUIT TART WITH ALMOND CREAM

This basic recipe for fruit tart can be used with virtually any fruit that takes your fancy. Soak the fruit in your favourite liqueur before placing on tart.

*250 g short crust pastry, baked for pie base*

### ALMOND CREAM

*1 tablespoon arrowroot*

*1¼ cups (300 ml/10 fl oz) milk*

*1 egg, lightly beaten*

*3 tablespoons caster sugar*

*50 g (1¾ oz) butter*

*50 g (1¾ oz) ground almonds*

### FRUIT FILLINGS

*500 g (16 oz) nectarines*

*500 g (16 oz) bananas*

*500 g (16 oz) strawberries, hulled*

Pour warm almond cream over cooked pastry which has cooled. Arrange fruit on top of almond cream. Refrigerate for an hour and serve.

**SERVES 6**

*Fruit Tart With Almond Cream*

# FIGS WITH HONEY CREAM

A wonderfully simple, easy recipe.

> *12 figs, peeled and sliced*
>
> *2 tablespoons brandy*
>
> *3 tablespoons orange juice*

## HONEY CREAM

> *3 tablespoons honey*
>
> *2 cups (500 ml/16 fl oz) cream, whipped*

Brush fig slices with combined brandy and orange juice.

*Figs with Honey Cream*

Fold honey through cream. Arrange figs and honey cream in layers in six individual serving dishes. Chill until required.

**SERVES 6**

# MAPLE FIGS

> *¾ cup (180 ml/6 fl oz) maple syrup*
>
> *½ cup (125 ml/4 fl oz) water*
>
> *1 cinnamon stick*
>
> *4 tablespoons brandy*
>
> *8 figs*

*Maple Figs*

Combine maple syrup, water, cinnamon stick and brandy in a saucepan over low heat.

Add figs and simmer for 5 minutes or until soft.

Cut figs in quarters and serve with maple sauce.

**SERVES 4**

# RASPBERRY MERINGUE HEARTS

**MERINGUE**

*250 g (8 oz) sugar*

*⅔ cup (170 ml/5½ fl oz) water*

*4 egg whites*

**FILLING**

*2 cups (500 ml/16 fl oz) cream, whipped*

*2 tablespoons brandy*

**TOPPING**

*500 g (1 lb) raspberries*

*icing sugar*

Preheat oven to 120°C (250°F).

To Make Meringue: Stir sugar and water in a saucepan over low heat until sugar dissolves. Brush sides of pan with a wet pastry brush to remove any sugar crystals. Simmer until syrup is thick and the temperature reaches 125°C (250°F) on a sugar thermometer. Remove from heat.

Beat egg whites until stiff peaks form. Gradually add sugar syrup in a thin stream. Beat continually until meringue cools.

Place meringue in a piping bag fitted with a plain nozzle. Mark 12 hearts on baking paper and place on baking trays. Pipe meringue on heart traces. Smooth with a palate knife. Bake meringues for 45 to 60 minutes or until dry and firm.

To Assemble: Place six hearts on serving plates. Fold cream and brandy together. Pipe over hearts. Top with raspberries and remaining heart meringues. Sprinkle with icing sugar and serve immediately.

**SERVES 6**

# SICILIAN CASSATA

This is a homely and delicious version of this most famous Sicilian sweet.

*700 g (22 oz) very fresh ricotta*

*200 g (6½ oz) sugar*

*4 tablespoons rum*

*150 g (5 oz) candied lemon peel*

*100 g (3½ oz) cooking chocolate, chopped into very small pieces*

*400 g (13 oz) sponge cake or sponge fingers*

If you wish to unmould the cassata, line the mould with greaseproof paper brushed with rum.

Using a large bowl and a wooden spoon, cream the ricotta until very smooth, add the sugar, 1 tablespoon rum, the candied peel and the chocolate. Sprinkle the remaining rum on the sponge cake (or sponge fingers) and line the bottom and sides of a mould or soufflé dish. Fill the mould with the ricotta mixture and refrigerate for at least three hours before serving.

**SERVES 6**

# CHILLED STRAWBERRY SOUFFLE

*6 eggs, separated*

*185 g (6 oz) sugar*

*500 g (1 lb) strawberries, hulled and pureed*

*2½ tablespoons gelatine*

*½ cup (125 ml/4 fl oz) boiling water*

*2 tablespoons grated orange rind*

*2½ cups (625 ml/20 fl oz) cream, whipped*

*3 tablespoons sugar, extra*

*grated chocolate*

*extra whipped cream*

Beat egg yolks and sugar in a bowl until thick and creamy. Fold through strawberry puree. Dissolve gelatine in boiling water in a small bowl. Fold through strawberry mixture with rind and cream.

Place a greased aluminium foil collar around a large souffle dish and secure with string.

Beat egg whites until stiff. Add extra sugar and beat until thick and glossy. Fold through strawberry mixture. Pour into soufflé dish. Chill for 6 hours or until set.

Decorate with grated chocolate and extra whipped cream.

**SERVES 8**

# CARAMELISED ORANGES

*200 g (6½ oz) sugar*

*40 g (1⅓ oz) butter*

*4 large oranges (navels)*

*4 tablespoons toasted slivered almonds*

Dissolve sugar over low heat, stirring constantly, and simmer until syrup is a golden colour. Remove from heat, add butter and stir until smooth. Peel the oranges, removing all pith and white membrane. Slice thinly and arrange on a serving dish in overlapping layers. Pour the sauce over them and sprinkle with almonds. Serve with whipped cream, if wished.

**SERVES 4**

*Raspberry Meringue Hearts*

# FROZEN BERRY MOUSSE

*4 egg yolks*

*375 g (12 oz) sugar*

*250 g (8 oz) mixed fresh or frozen berries*

*3 tablespoons Cointreau liqueur*

*2 cups (500 ml/16 fl oz) cream, whipped*

*extra berries and cream*

Beat egg yolks and sugar in a bowl over a saucepan of simmering water until thick and fluffy. Process berries in a food processor until smooth. Stir berries through a sieve to remove seeds.

*Frozen Berry Mousse*

Fold berry puree through egg mixture with liqueur and cream. Pour into an oiled mould. Freeze overnight or until set.

To Serve: Soften slightly. Invert onto a serving plate. Serve with extra berries and cream.

**SERVES 4 TO 6**

# BRAISED BERRIES

*2 tablespoons Galliano*

*2 tablespoons white rum*

*½ cup (125 ml/4 fl oz) water*

*2 tablespoons sugar*

*1 tablespoon lemon juice*

*2 teaspoons arrowroot*

*Braised Berries*

*150 g (5 oz) strawberries, hulled*

*150 g (5 oz) raspberries*

*150 g (5 oz) blueberries*

*cream*

Simmer Galliano, rum, water and sugar in a small saucepan over low heat.

Blend together lemon juice and arrowroot. Add to saucepan and stir until mixture thickens.

Add berries and cook for 1 minute. Serve in bowls with cream.

**SERVES 4**

# POACHED TAMARILLOS WITH LIME BAKED CUSTARDS

250 g (8 oz) sugar
4 cups (1 litre/32 fl oz) water
16 tamarillos

### LIME BAKED CUSTARDS

2 eggs
2 tablespoons sugar
1½ cups (375 ml/12 fl oz) milk
2 teaspoons grated lime rind
2 tablespoons lime juice
icing sugar

Preheat oven to 160°C (325°F).

To Prepare Tamarillos: Stir sugar and water in a large saucepan over low heat until sugar dissolves. Add tamarillos and poach for 6 minutes. Remove from pan and peel. Return to pan. Cook for a further 4 minutes or until soft. Cut almost in half, leaving stem end intact.

To Make Custards: Beat together eggs and sugar in a bowl until thick and fluffy. Mix in milk, rind and juice. Pour mixture into eight small ovenproof pots. Place pots in a baking dish half filled with water. Bake for 10 to 12 minutes or until set. Sprinkle custards with icing sugar. Place on a serving plate beside two tamarillos.

SERVES 8

*Poached Tamarillos with Lime Baked Custards*

# BERRY CHARLOTTE

## CHARLOTTE

20 to 25 sponge finger biscuits

6 egg yolks

125 g (4 oz) sugar

1½ cups (375 ml/12 fl oz) milk

½ teaspoon vanilla essence

2 teaspoons gelatine

3 tablespoons boiling water

½ cup (125 ml/4 fl oz) sour cream

½ cup (125 ml/4 fl oz) thickened cream

## BERRY COULIS

500 g (1 lb) fresh or frozen berries

2 teaspoons sugar

2 tablespoons kirsch

To Make Charlotte: Line a large charlotte mould or cake tin with sponge fingers. Trim biscuits to fit evenly and tightly into tin.

Beat egg yolks and sugar in a bowl until thick and fluffy. Heat milk and vanilla in a small saucepan until hot. Whisk into egg mixture.

Return to saucepan. Stir over low heat until mixture thickens.

Dissolve gelatine in boiling water in a small bowl. Add to custard mixture. Whip creams together and fold into custard. Cool custard slightly before pouring into mould.

Refrigerate for 6 hours or until set. Invert onto a serving plate and tie with ribbon to secure shape.

To Make Berry Coulis: Process berries in a food processor until smooth. Stir berry mixture through a sieve. Stir through sugar and kirsch. Serve with charlotte.

**SERVES 10**

# PEACH AND LIME TART

## BASE

125 g (4 oz) butter

2 tablespoons caster sugar

155 g (5 oz) plain flour

1 tablespoon lime rind

1 egg, lightly beaten

## FILLING

3 eggs

90 g (3 oz) caster sugar

5 large peaches, peeled and chopped

375 g (12 oz) ricotta cheese

1 tablespoon lime juice

extra cream and peaches

Preheat oven to 180°C (350°F).

To Make Base: Process butter, sugar, flour, rind and egg in a food processor to form a soft dough. A little cold water may be needed.

Wrap dough in plastic wrap and refrigerate for 30 minutes. Roll out dough to fit a 25 cm (10 in) springform tart tin. Prick base of pastry and bake for 10 minutes or until golden.

To Make Filling: Process eggs, sugar, peaches, ricotta and lime juice in a food processor until smooth. Pour into tart shell. Bake for 35 to 45 minutes or until firm.

Chill and serve with extra cream and peaches.

**SERVES 8**

# BAKED FRUITS STEEPED IN ALCOHOL

## SUGGESTED COMBINATIONS

This recipe is more a concept for you to experiment with than a specific recipe and accompaniments. Try the fruits suggested here or choose other fruits in season and add your favourite liqueurs.

plums in port

apples in tokay or muscat

rhubarb in cassis

hot bananas in brandy

oranges in Grand Marnier

citrus zest

fruit juice

sugar

spices

Preheat oven to 190°C (375°F).

Prepare fruit of your choice and place in an ovenproof dish. Sprinkle with citrus zest, fruit juice, sugar (or honey), spices and then the alcohol. Bake for 15 to 20 minutes and serve with generous spoonfuls of whipped cream.

---

### COOKING WITH ALCOHOL

Alcohol is often the secret ingredient in a recipe. The alcohol is burnt off during the cooking process, leaving the flavour but not the potency. However, when alcohol is used to soak fruit, for example, which is served without cooking, the potency should be taken into consideration. A flambé is a wonderfully fun way of enjoying the flavour of your favourite spirit. Try a flambé with your Christmas pudding. Heat brandy in a small saucepan, pour over the hot pudding and ignite.

---

# Fruit in Season

| Produce | Southern Hemisphere | Northern Hemisphere |
| --- | --- | --- |
| Apples (Delicious) | All year | All year |
| Apples (Red) (Jonathan, Rome, Beauty, Bonza) | March to December | October to March |
| Apples (Green) (Granny Smith) | All year | All year |
| Apricots | November to February | June to August |
| Avocadoes (Alligator Pears) | All year | All year |
| Bananas | All year | All year |
| Blackberries | January to March | August to September |
| Boysenberries | December to February | July to August |
| Cherries | October to mid January | May to July |
| Custard Apple | April to August | June to December |
| Carambola (Star Fruit) | October to July | June to July |
| Coconuts | All year | All year |
| Dates | All year | All year |
| Feijoas | May to August | All year |
| Figs, Fresh | December to May | July to September |
| Gooseberries | October to February | June to July |
| Grapefruit | All year | All year |
| Grapes (Early Varieties) | November | All year |
| Grapes (Black Muscat) | December to April | July to May |
| Grapes (White/Black Varieties) | January to June | All year |
| Grapes (Sultanas) | January to May | June to July/January to February |
| Guava | November to May | All year |
| Honeydew | All year | February to December |
| Kiwi Fruit (Chinese Gooseberry) | All year | All year |
| Lemons | All year | All year |
| Limes | June to September | All year |
| Lychees (litchis) | November to March | December to March |

| Produce | Southern Hemisphere | Northern Hemisphere |
|---|---|---|
| Mandarins (Clementines, Tangerines, Satsuma) | April to October | July to February |
| Mangoes | November to March | All year |
| Mulberries | October to December | June to September |
| Oranges (Navels) | May to October | November to March/May to July |
| Oranges (Valencia) | September to April | April to November |
| Pawpaw (Papaya) | All year | All year |
| Passionfruit (Purple Granadilla) | All year | All year |
| Peaches | November to March | May to September/December to January |
| Pears | All year | All year |
| Persimmons (Kaki Fruit, Sharon Fruit, Apple of the Orient) | February to June | October to December |
| Pineapples | All year | All year |
| Plums (Early Varieties) | December | July to April |
| Plums (Wilsons) | November to December | July to April |
| Plums (Blood & others) | December to February | July to April |
| Plums (President) | March to May | July to April |
| Quinces | January to May | Mid July |
| Raspberries | November to February | July to August |
| Redcurrants, Blackcurrants | December | June to September |
| Rhubarb | All year | January to September |
| Rockmelon | All year | July to September |
| Strawberries | All year | June to July |
| Strawberries (Imported) | May to July | All year |
| Rambutans | September to May | All year |
| Tamarillo | March to December | August to September |
| Watermelon | All year | May to September |

Plate from Waterford Wedgwood,
fabric from I Redelman and Son

# A Cool Change

*E*scape from the summer sun to a cool shady spot and spoil yourself with these refreshingly chilly desserts. Homemade ice creams and sorbets are easy to prepare and will bring a cool change to those long hot days.

# Making Perfect Home-Made Ice Cream

*F*ew things in life taste better than a scoop of home-made ice cream or a fresh fruity sorbet. Why not indulge yourself, your family and friends with delicious iced desserts using natural, nutritious ingredients, an ice cream maker and a little time?

Most recipes can be simply and easily prepared at home with a time-saving ice cream maker, whilst others only need to be still-frozen just the way our grandmas made their iced delights.

## WHAT'S SO GOOD ABOUT IT?

It is all natural. You don't need any additives to extend shelf life: your confections are unlikely to have a shelf life! If home-made ice cream lasts a day, you'll be lucky.

Tasting good isn't enough in these health-conscious days. What you eat has to be good for you, too. Ice cream and iced desserts prepared with fresh milk, cream, eggs and fruit plus nuts and honey are very nutritious. Bursting with natural ingredients, these foods can play a useful part in a healthy diet.

## WEIGHT WATCHING

Ice creams and diets aren't mutually exclusive. They can be eaten in moderation by people trying to lose weight. One scoop of vanilla ice cream (custard-style) contains about 574 kJ (140 calories) whereas a standard, fruity-flavoured carton of yoghurt contains about 838 kJ (210 calories).

## Milkfat Content of Cream

| Type of Cream | Percentage of milkfat (minimum) |
| --- | --- |
| AUSTRALIA | |
| Reduced cream | 25% |
| Cream | 35% |
| Thickened cream | 35% |
| Whipping cream | 40% (Qld) |
| | 42% (WA) |
| Rich cream | 48% (Vic, WA, SA, Tas) |
| | |
| UK | |
| Single cream | 18% |
| Whipping cream | 35% |
| Double cream | 48% |

*Pictured on previous pages: Passionfruit Granita (page 79), Praline Ice Cream with Chocolate Fudge Sauce (page 83)*

## THE ESSENTIAL INGREDIENTS

The ingredients are all natural — cream or milk, eggs and sugar in ice cream; fruits and egg whites in sorbets and sherbets.

### Cream

Rich ice cream is usually cream based. There are several different types of cream available labelled according to the amount of milkfat that they contain.

Most of the recipes in this book that require cream, use cream containing 35 per cent milkfat. In those recipes calling for milk, you can make a creamier version by substituting cream for some of the milk content. To make a drier, firmer ice cream, slightly reduce the amount of cream and egg yolks.

### Milk

Recipes using milk make a harder and more crystalline dessert than those with cream. The type of milk you choose affects the flavour. The recipes in this book were prepared using homogenised pasteurised milk. If you substitute skimmed milk, your ice cream will be icier. Buttermilk also has less fat but is thick and has a refreshing acidity that blends well with many fruit ices.

For vegetarians, soya bean milk is ideal. It is low in kilojoules and cholesterol-free. Yoghurt makes a slightly piquant flavoured ice on its own or blended with milk, creams or even soft cheeses.

Tofu is another substitute popular with vegetarians and people cutting down on cholesterol and kilojoules. It is low in fat and high in protein. Some varieties have a coarse texture. Choose a creamy smooth brand like Silken Tofu for making ice creams.

### Sugar

If you freeze a litre (32 fl oz) of cream, it will be rock hard and impossible to serve. Sugar in some form is essential. It not only sweetens the flavour but controls the softness of your ice cream. Too much and your ice cream won't freeze; too little and you may need a pick axe. Undissolved sugar will give the ice cream a grainy texture.

Granulated sugar and caster sugar are used in most recipes. Liquid sweeteners such as honey or maple syrup give ice creams a flavour all their own. In some recipes, the kilojoule conscious can substitute artificial sweeteners. As a rough guide, three or four sweeteners equal about 25 g (¾ oz) of sugar. It's worth remembering that artificial sweeteners lose some of their sweetness when heated, so it's a good idea to add them after any cooking.

## ICE CREAM MAKERS

An ice cream maker continually churns as it freezes, aerating the mixture and preventing ice crystals from forming.

If you haven't already succumbed and bought a machine, now is the time to weigh up the pros and cons. They do produce the smoothest ice cream in the shortest time but to make the most of your investment, it's important to use it fairly often.

Several types are available, from the top-of-the-range domestic models with a built-in freezing unit, fixed bowl and removable bowls for extra batches; to the popularly priced models, either those with a removable dish you freeze before churning or the small electric models with a rechargeable battery that churn the ice cream inside your own freezer.

Before buying, check the features of each type. Look at the noise level, the amount of ice cream you could make in a day, the preparation time (recharging the battery or freezing the dish) and ease of cleaning. One feature to look for, particularly, is a paddle that lifts clear of the ice cream before it freezes hard.

## HOW GOOD IS STILL-FREEZING?

You don't necessarily need modern labour saving devices. Still-freezing makes absolutely delicious ice cream if you beat it correctly. Continual and regular stirring is needed to prevent the formation of ice crystals and speed freezing. Simply stir two or three times during freezing time by beating the edges of the mixture into the centre with a fork or rotary hand beater.

## HOW LONG TO FREEZE?

There's no easy answer to this question. The time depends on the type of ice cream maker, the temperature of your equipment, whether you chilled the ingredients, the weather, the temperature in your kitchen, the quantity of ice cream and even the shape of your container. Manufacturers give approximate times in their ice cream maker manuals. For still-freezing, allow two to three hours. To avoid the disappointment of half frozen ices, make them the day before you need them, allowing time for the flavours to ripen and the texture to form properly.

## EQUIPMENT

- Measuring jug, cup and spoon
- Scales are a must. Always weigh or measure out the ingredients, especially sugar
- A double boiler (for custard making)
- Utensils such as wooden spoons, spatula and nylon sieve
- An electric blender
- Metal or plastic containers with lids for freezing and storing the ice creams
- A decorative serving container for those iced desserts like mousses, parfaits and soufflés, which go straight from freezer to table.

## FREEZING TIPS

- Chill your equipment — bowls, whisks, spatulas — before use.
- Cool your custard-base mixture quickly by plunging the bowl into a basin of cold water or ice cubes.
- Chill all other mixtures in the refrigerator before placing in ice cream maker.
- Turn the setting of your freezer to its coldest or quick freeze position.
- Metal containers will freeze ice creams etc faster than plastic. But don't use metal with acid fruits as the acid will react.
- Ice cream will still-freeze faster in a shallow, metal container.
- If using the freezer, place one side of the container in touch with the freezer sides or base. Leave space for the air to circulate around the container.
- Home-made ice cream should be made and frozen at least a day before eating to allow the ice cream to set and ripen.
- Ice cream should always be removed from the freezer and kept in the fridge for 30 minutes to allow slow softening before serving.

## FRUIT AND ICES

Fruit and ices must surely be among most people's favourite desserts. The early frozen ices were made from fruits before the invention of ice-cream. Ices have a very long history and were probably invented by the ancient Chinese who made a kind of sherbet by mixing together snow and fresh fruit.

Although you can now buy many good varieties of commercially produced ices, it is much more rewarding to make your own. You will be surprised by the difference in flavour and texture, and your family will love you for it. Ices fall into several different categories:

- Water ices are made from fruit juice, sugar and water. Sherbets, sorbets, granitas and marquises are all types of water ice. They are all made from a flavoured sugar syrup. You can use wine or liqueurs to flavour these ices as well as fresh fruit. Granitas are the coarse Italian ices while sorbets are much smoother and almost opaque.
- Ice-creams can be made by many different methods. Most are made from a milk custard but parfaits use only egg yolks and syrup. Ice-creams are often mixed with fruits, sauces, meringue, nuts and cream to make a delicious sundae. They are served in tall glasses and always delight adults and children alike.

## Making Ice Cream

Tip into a chilled container

Well-timed beating aerates the ice cream better than using a food processor

Return the mixture to freezer to firm again

Place in a serving dish

Some ice-creams make ideal desserts for dinner parties and always look spectacular. A glamorous bombe or fruity cassata will impress your guests and make a refreshing end to a meal. A bombe is always made in a special dome-shaped mould and has the advantage that it can be made and frozen well in advance and decorated just before you serve it.

## SAUCES AND GARNISHES

You can upstage ice-cream by serving it with a special sauce or garnish. Hot or chilled sauces made with fruit or liqueurs are particularly good. If you don't have time to make a sauce, just sprinkle over some chopped nuts, toasted almonds, grated chocolate, crumbled meringues or macaroons,

chopped fresh fruit such as peaches, raspberries, strawberries, pears and bananas, mixed dried fruit soaked in liqueur, or melted jam.

Other ideas for toppings include crushed peanut brittle, toasted coconut, melted chocolate (especially chocolate caramel bars), chopped preserved ginger and crumbled biscuits.

# ECONOMICAL ICE CREAM

*1½ teaspoons gelatine*

*1 cup (250 ml/8 fl oz) boiling water*

*1 cup (250 ml/8 fl oz) cold water*

*2 cups (500 ml/16 fl oz) evaporated milk*

*175 g (5¾ oz) non-fat milk powder*

*100 g (3½ oz) caster sugar*

*1 teaspoon flavouring essence*

Dissolve the gelatine in the boiling water, in a large mixing bowl. Add the cold water, evaporated milk, milk powder and sugar. Beat thoroughly until it forms a smooth creamy mixture (this can be done with an electric mixer). Freeze until firm.

Remove from the freezer and leave to stand until it is softened a little. Pour into the mixing bowl and mash. Beat quickly until the mixture is light and fluffy and has doubled in size. Add the flavouring essence and place in freezer trays. Freeze until firm.

**MAKES ABOUT 1½ LITRES (2½ PINTS)**

# FRESH FRUIT ICE CREAM

This recipe is suitable for any type of fresh fruit. Soft fruit should be freshly sieved and hard fruit should be cooked, cooled and sieved. For 2 cups (500 ml/16 fl oz) of fruit pulp you will need about 1 kg (2 lb) stoneless fruits (strawberries, raspberries, cranberries, gooseberries etc), and a little more for fruits with stones.

*2 cups (500 ml/16 fl oz) fresh fruit pulp*

*juice ½ lemon*

*juice ½ orange*

*225 g (7½ oz) sugar*

*150 ml (5 fl oz) water*

*150 ml (5 fl oz) double cream*

Mix the fruit pulp with the lemon and orange juice.

Place the sugar and water in a pan and stir over a gentle heat until dissolved. Bring to the boil and boil for 5 minutes without stirring. Leave to cool.

Add the cold sugar syrup to the fruit mixture. Whip the cream until it is just thick and fold into the fruit mixture. Transfer to a freezer tray and freeze until firm.

**SERVES 6 TO 8**

# REAL VANILLA ICE CREAM

*2 cups (500 ml/16 fl oz) milk*

*1 vanilla bean, split lengthways*

*200 g (6½ oz) caster sugar*

*6 egg yolks*

*1 cup (250 ml/8 fl oz) cream*

Heat milk, vanilla and half the sugar in a saucepan until boiling. Cover and stand for 15 minutes.

Beat egg yolks in a bowl with remaining sugar until light and fluffy.

Bring the milk back to the boil. Cool slightly and whisk in egg mixture. Cook over low heat until mixture forms a thin custard and coats the back of a spoon.

Remove vanilla. Cool custard. Whip cream until firm and fold through cooled custard. Pour into an ice cream maker. Follow the manufacturer's instructions.

**SERVES 6**

Vanilla was first discovered by the Aztecs. The long, yellow pods of the vanilla orchid are picked before ripening and undergo a curing process. The cured pods are dark brown in appearance and have a sweet and fragrant aroma. Using vanilla beans or pods is preferable in cooking as they have a superior flavour to vanilla essence. Vanilla beans or pods can be used to flavour sweet and baked goods then washed and dried and used again several times.

# PASSIONFRUIT AND PISTACHIO ICE CREAM

*250 g (8 oz) shelled pistachio nuts*
*200 g (6½ oz) sugar*
*3 cups (750 ml/24 fl oz) milk*
*6 egg yolks*
*3 to 4 passionfruit, halved*

Process pistachio nuts and half the sugar in a food processor until finely chopped. Heat milk in a saucepan and bring to the boil.

Place egg yolks and remaining sugar in a bowl. Beat until thick and fluffy. Whisk into milk. Stir over low heat until mixture forms a thin custard that coats the back of a spoon.

Stir through pistachio mixture and passionfruit pulp. Cool.

Pour into an ice cream maker. Follow the manufacturer's instructions.

**SERVES 6 TO 8**

# RUM AND RAISIN ICE CREAM

*100 g (3½ oz) raisins*
*¾ cup (180 ml/6 fl oz) dark rum*
*100 ml (3½ fl oz) boiling water*
*1 egg*
*600 ml (20 fl oz) cream*
*½ cup (125 ml/4 fl oz) milk*
*⅔ cup (150 g/5 oz) sugar*
*1 tablespoon vanilla essence*

Place raisins, rum and water in a bowl and set aside for 30 minutes. Drain liquid and reserve.

Beat together reserved liquid, egg, cream, milk, sugar and vanilla in a bowl.

Pour mixture into an ice cream maker. Follow the manufacturer's instructions. Add raisins when ice cream is half frozen.

**SERVES 8**

---

### ICE CREAM FUN

Children love ice cream.
Fill small dishes with all of the things they love — hundreds and thousands, soft lollies, wafers, yummy sauces — and let them make their own sundaes. Alternatively, add a scoop of ice cream to milk and fresh fruit of your choice and process in the blender for an instant health shake.

---

# COFFEE AND HAZELNUT ICE CREAM

*6 egg yolks*
*150 g (5 oz) sugar*
*2 cups (500 ml/16 fl oz) milk*
*1 cup (250 ml/8 fl oz) cream*
*100 ml (3½ fl oz) coffee liqueur*
*125 g (4 oz) toasted hazelnuts, chopped*

Place egg yolks and sugar in a bowl over a saucepan of simmering water. Beat until light and fluffy.

In a separate pan, heat milk until hot. Pour into egg mixture. Stir until mixture forms a thin custard that coats the back of a spoon. Remove from heat. Stir in cream, coffee liqueur and hazelnuts.

Pour into an ice cream maker. Follow the manufacturer's instructions.

**SERVES 6**

---

### SERVING DISHES

Ice creams with interesting colours and inclusions like fruit or nuts look great served in tall glasses or glass bowls.

---

# FROZEN RASPBERRY YOGHURT

*2 tablespoons grated lemon rind*

*155 g (5 oz) raspberries, crushed*

*375 g (12 oz) sugar*

*4 cups (1 litre/32 fl oz) yoghurt*

Combine rind, raspberries, sugar and yoghurt in a bowl.

Pour into an ice cream maker. Follow the manufacturer's instructions.

**SERVES 6 TO 8**

# BRANDIED MASCARPONE ICE

This ice cream tastes delicious served with poached fruit and almond cookies.

*4 egg yolks*

*175 g (5¾ oz) icing sugar*

*500 g (1 lb) mascarpone cheese*

*3 tablespoons brandy*

Beat egg yolks and sugar in a bowl until thick. Gradually add mascarpone, while still beating. Stir through brandy.

Pour into a metal container and freeze overnight.

Before serving, soften in refrigerator for 30 minutes.

**SERVES 6**

*Frozen Raspberry Yoghurt and Brandied Mascarpone Ice*

# LIME AND MINT SORBET

A very refreshing dessert

*250 g (8 oz) sugar*

*1 cup (250 ml/8 fl oz) water*

*1 cup (250 ml/8 fl oz) lime juice*

*¾ cup (185 ml/6 fl oz) water, extra*

*2 tablespoons chopped fresh mint*

Stir sugar and water in a saucepan over low heat until sugar dissolves. Bring to the boil and boil for 2 minutes. Remove from heat and cool.

Add lime juice, extra water and mint to sugar syrup.

Pour into an ice cream maker. Follow the manufacturer's instructions or pour mixture into a metal container and freeze for 1 hour. Beat sorbet to break up ice crystals. Repeat this procedure twice.

**SERVES 6**

## LIME

The lime is one of the smaller of the citrus fruits and is grown mainly in tropical countries. The small thin-skinned fruit is of Indian origin and is closely related to the lemon. Limes are used for their juice and their finely grated peel. Limes are often used as substitutes for lemons.

# ROSE GERANIUM SORBET

This is a favourite dessert, ideal to serve with curries when entertaining. Growing rose geraniums just outside your kitchen on a sunny deck or patio is easy and extremely useful. Added to a refreshing lemon sorbet, a few leaves turn the sorbet a beautiful pale green and have the most wonderful perfume and flavour.

*185 g (6 oz) sugar*

*2½ cups (600 ml/20 fl oz) water*

*6 lemons*

*4 (6 if small) rose geranium leaves, crumpled*

*1 egg white*

*extra leaves, for decoration*

Place sugar in a medium-sized saucepan with water. Grate over lemon rind. Heat over low heat and when sugar has dissolved, bring to the boil. Add crushed leaves. Boil for 6 minutes. Cool.

Squeeze juice from the lemons and strain into cooled syrup. Pour mixture into cold freezer trays or a metal bowl. Place in a freezer until mixture just begins to freeze. Remove, turn into a bowl and discard geranium leaves. Beat with a whisk until smooth, but not melted. Beat egg white until stiff but not dry, fold lightly through mixture and return to tray. Cover and freeze until firm.

Pile sorbet into chilled glasses and serve decorated with a rose geranium flower and leaves.

**SERVES 2 TO 4**

# PINEAPPLE GRANITA

*185 g (6 oz) sugar*

*1½ cups (375 ml/12 fl oz) water*

*900 g (2 lb) pineapple*

*2 tablespoons lemon juice*

*2 tablespoons orange juice*

Stir sugar and water in a small saucepan over low heat until sugar dissolves.

Bring to the boil. Simmer without stirring for 2 minutes. Cool.

Place pineapple, lemon and orange juice in a food processor. Process until smooth. Add sugar syrup and process for 30 seconds.

Pour into a metal container. Freeze for 2 to 3 hours, stirring occasionally.

**SERVES 6**

# WATERMELON GRANITA

*125 g (4 oz) sugar*

*⅔ cup (160 ml/5½ fl oz) boiling water*

*1 kg (2 lb) watermelon, peeled, seeded and chopped*

*2 tablespoons lemon juice*

Place sugar in a bowl and pour over boiling water. Stir to dissolve sugar.

Process watermelon in a food processor until smooth. Combine with dissolved sugar. Pour into a large shallow tin.

Freeze for 30 minutes then whisk to break ice crystals. Return to freezer for 1 hour and whisk again.

Before serving, soften in refrigerator for 10 minutes then mash with a fork to form a slushy ice.

**SERVES 4**

# Sorbets and Granitas

$S$orbets (sometimes called sherbets) and granitas are frozen ices. Granitas have a coarser grain, sorbets a smoother grain. The sugar in these ices is included to prevent them freezing too much or too little, so care should be taken with measurements.

# PASSIONFRUIT GRANITA

*8 passionfruit, halved*

*1½ cups (375 ml/12 fl oz) mango nectar*

*125 g (4 oz) caster sugar*

*3 tablespoons lemon juice*

Scoop pulp from passionfruit. Combine with mango nectar, sugar and lemon juice in a bowl.

Freeze in a lamington or large tin for 30 minutes. Remove from freezer and whisk to break up ice crystals.

Return to freezer and freeze for 1 hour. Whisk again.

Before serving, soften in refrigerator for 10 minutes then mash with a fork to make a slushy ice.

**SERVES 4**

## SORBETS

Sorbets are often served to cleanse the palate between courses, but it is a shame to limit their use. The recipes here show how many fantastic types of sorbets there are. Shine the spotlight on them by including them in your dessert repertoire.

# RASPBERRY ICE CREAM

*1 cup (250 ml/8 fl oz) cream*

*1 cup (250 ml/8 fl oz) milk*

*5 egg yolks*

*125 g (4 oz) sugar*

*250 g (8 oz) raspberries, pureed and sieved*

Heat cream and milk in a saucepan until boiling. Remove from heat.

Beat together egg yolks and sugar in a large bowl until thick and fluffy. Whisk in cream mixture and pureed raspberries. Cool.

*Raspberry Ice Cream*

Place in an ice cream maker. Follow the manufacturers instructions.

**SERVES 6**

# CAFE LATTE GELATO

To add flavour and a crunchy texture, serve with chocolate coated coffee beans.

*½ cup (125 ml/4 fl oz) very strong espresso coffee*

*2½ cups (625 ml/20 fl oz) milk*

*90 g (3 oz) caster sugar*

*1 teaspoon vanilla essence*

*Cafe Latte Gelato*

Combine coffee, milk, sugar and vanilla in a bowl.

Pour mixture into an ice cream maker. Follow the manufacturer's instructions.

**SERVES 6**

## QUICK LEMON SYLLABUB

A syllabub is whipped flavoured cream.

*4 tablespoons dry white wine*

*finely-grated rind and juice of 1 large lemon*

*2½ tablespoons caster sugar*

*1¼ cups (300 ml/10 fl oz) cream*

Put the wine, lemon rind and juice and sugar into a bowl. Stir to blend the ingredients, then pour in the cream and whisk until the mixture is light and thick. Pour the syllabub into individual goblets and chill well. Serve with sponge fingers, if wished.

**SERVES 2**

---

### STIRRING ICES

Halfway through the freezing process, frozen ices should be removed from the freezer and beaten to break up the ice crystals. Don't do this too soon or the mixture will liquidise.

---

## FROZEN YOGHURT AMBROSIA

The topping can be made well in advance and stored in an airtight jar.

*⅔ cup (150 ml/5 fl oz) cream*

*110 g (3½ oz) caster sugar*

*1 teaspoon vanilla essence*

*1 cup (250 ml/8 fl oz) natural yoghurt*

### TOPPING

*3 tablespoons sunflower seeds*

*3 tablespoons chopped hazelnuts*

*3 tablespoons roughly chopped walnuts*

*1 tablespoon desiccated coconut*

*75 g (2½ oz) dried apple rings, roughly chopped*

*75 g (2½ oz) dried peaches or apricots, roughly chopped*

Whip the cream until it is just thick, and fold in the sugar, vanilla and yoghurt. Transfer the mixture into a freezer container and place it in the freezer for 1 to 2 hours, until the mixture is icy around the edges. Whisk until smooth, then return to the freezer until firm.

To Make Topping: Lightly toast the sunflower seeds and mix with the remaining topping ingredients. Allow the ice cream to soften in the refrigerator for 30 minutes before serving. Scoop the ice cream into dessert glasses and sprinkle with the topping. Serve immediately.

**SERVES 4 TO 6**

## FROMAGE BLANC

*150 g (5 oz) cottage cheese*

*185 g (6 oz) natural yoghurt*

*4 teaspoons lemon juice*

Combine all ingredients and blend until mixture is smooth and thick, like whipped cream. Cover and store in refrigerator for about 12 hours before using.

**MAKES ABOUT 1 ½ CUPS (375 ML/12 FL OZ)**

## LEMON LIME SHERBET

*250 g (8 oz) sugar*

*1 cup (250 ml/8 fl oz) water*

*2 tablespoons lemon juice*

*2 tablespoons lime juice*

*1 tablespoon grated lemon rind*

*1 tablespoon grated lime rind*

*2 egg whites*

Stir sugar and water in a saucepan over low heat until sugar dissolves.

Add lemon and lime juice and lemon and lime rind. Leave to cool.

Pour mixture into an ice cream maker. Follow the manufacturer's instructions. Do not allow mixture to become too set.

Beat egg whites until soft peaks form. Fold through softened mixture. Refreeze until set.

**SERVES 4**

# FROZEN IRISH COFFEE MOUSSE

*3 egg yolks*

*125 g (4 oz) sugar*

*1 tablespoon instant coffee, dissolved in 1 tablespoon hot water*

*1 cup (250 ml/8 fl oz) cream, whipped*

*1 tablespoon Irish whiskey*

*1½ cups (375 ml/12 fl oz) fromage blanc (see recipe)*

*1 tablespoon honey*

*½ teaspoon vanilla essence*

*2 egg whites*

Whisk egg yolks, sugar and dissolved coffee in a bowl over a pan of hot water until light and creamy and sugar dissolved. Remove and continue to whisk until cool. Fold in whiskey and cream.

Blend fromage blanc, honey and vanilla essence. Add to mousse. Whip egg whites until firm but not stiff and fold into mixture. Pour into metal tray. Leave until almost set, turn into bowl and whisk to increase volume. Return to tray and allow to freeze 1 hour before serving.

To Prepare Topping: Pour 1 cup black coffee into metal tray and freeze. As it freezes, fork around to form tiny crystals. When frozen sprinkle these on top of mousse to serve.

**SERVES 6 TO 8**

# PRALINE ICE CREAM WITH CHOCOLATE FUDGE SAUCE

*375 g (12 oz) sugar*

*¾ cup (180 ml/6 fl oz) hot water*

*90 g (3 oz) toasted slivered almonds*

*4 cups (1 litre/32 fl oz) vanilla ice cream*

*Chocolate Fudge Sauce (see recipe, page 20)*

Stir sugar and water in a saucepan over low heat until sugar dissolves. Bring to the boil and cook for 5 minutes or until a golden colour.

Place almonds on a greased oven tray and pour over toffee. Leave to set. Chop into small pieces.

Soften ice cream in a bowl. Mix through half the praline.

Line six star shaped moulds with plastic wrap. Spoon ice cream into moulds. Freeze until hard.

Unmould ice creams, sprinkle with extra praline and serve with Chocolate Fudge Sauce.

**SERVES 6**

# COCONUT PINEAPPLE GELATO

*2 cups (500 ml/16 fl oz) pineapple juice*

*1 cup (250 ml/8 fl oz) coconut cream*

*1 cup (250 ml/8 fl oz) milk*

*125 g (4 oz) sugar*

*3 tablespoons lime juice*

Combine pineapple juice, coconut cream, milk, sugar and lime juice in a bowl. Mix well to dissolve sugar.

Place in an ice cream maker. Follow the manufacturer's instructions.

**SERVES 4 TO 6**

## COCONUT CREAM

You can make your own coconut cream by shredding fresh coconut into a bowl and covering it with water. Allow it to stand overnight in the refrigerator. Strain the mixture and press the flesh in a sieve or in muslin to extract any extra cream.

# BLUEBERRY
# ICE CREAM

2 cups (250 g/8 oz) blueberries

4 cups (1 litre/32 fl oz) cream

9 egg yolks

250 g (8 oz) sugar

¼ cup (60 ml/2 fl oz) orange
   liqueur

Roughly chop blueberries and set
aside. Heat cream in a saucepan until
boiling. Add blueberries.

Beat egg yolks and sugar in a large
bowl until light and fluffy. Add hot
cream and combine well. Stir
through liqueur.

Pour into an ice cream maker.
Follow the manufacturer's
instructions.

**SERVES 8 TO 10**

# LAVENDER
# ICE CREAM

2 tablespoons fresh lavender
   flowers

1 vanilla bean

2 teaspoons grated lemon rind

2 cups (500 ml/16 fl oz) cream

2 cups (500 ml/16 fl oz) milk

4 eggs, lightly beaten

1 cup (250 g/8 oz) sugar

Place lavender, vanilla, rind, cream
and milk in a bowl. Cover and
refrigerate overnight. Strain and
discard lavender.

Heat the strained liquid in a saucepan
until almost boiling.

Beat eggs and sugar in a bowl until
light and fluffy. Pour hot liquid over
eggs and sugar while beating.

Return to pan. Stir over low heat
until mixture thickens and coats the
back of a spoon. Cool.

Pour into an ice cream maker.
Follow the manufacturer's
instructions.

**SERVES 8**

*Left: Blueberry Ice Cream*
*Below: Lavender Ice Cream*

# TAMARILLO ICE CREAM

*250 g (8 oz) sugar*

*1 cup (250 ml/8 fl oz) water*

*4 tamarillos*

*1¼ cups (450 ml/14 fl oz) cream*

*3 egg yolks*

Stir sugar and water in a saucepan over low heat until sugar dissolves. Boil syrup for 5 minutes.

Add tamarillos. Simmer for 4 to 6 minutes or until soft.

Remove tamarillos from pan and peel. Process tamarillos in a food processor until smooth. Sieve to remove seeds.

Heat cream and egg yolks in a saucepan over low heat and stir until thickened slightly. Add to tamarillo puree.

Pour into an ice cream maker. Follow the manufacturer's instructions.

**SERVES 4**

# LEMON DELICIOUS ICE CREAM

*4 cups (1 litre/32 fl oz) vanilla ice cream*

*250 g (8 oz) good quality lemon curd (see recipe, page 28)*

*2 tablespoons lemon juice*

*brandy snap baskets or chocolate cups*

Place ice cream in a bowl. Mix through lemon curd and juice. Refreeze until required.

To serve, place scoops of ice cream in brandy snap baskets or chocolate cups, either home-made or bought from cake and sweet shops.

**SERVES 6**

## CHOCOLATE CUPS

Melt chocolate in a bowl over simmering water. Lightly brush the inside of individual tart tins with oil. Spoon melted chocolate into the bottom of each. Using a pastry brush, spread chocolate evenly around the base and sides of tin. Allow to set in the refrigerator. Repeat the process if the cases are too thin. When solid, lift from tins carefully.

## BRANDY SNAP BASKETS

To make brandy snap baskets melt 60 g (2 oz) of butter, 45 g (1½ oz) brown sugar and 90 g (3 oz) golden syrup in a small saucepan. Heat until sugar has dissolved. Cool. Stir 30 g (1 oz) plain flour into the cooled mixture. Place teaspoonfuls of the mixture onto greased baking trays. Bake at 180°C (350°F) until golden (about 5 to 10 minutes). Allow to cool slightly. Remove from tray and place over a greased up-turned glass. Shape into a basket shape and allow to cool completely.

# BRANDY AND APPLE ICE

*2 large apples, peeled and chopped*

*2 tablespoons water*

*1½ cups (375 ml/12 fl oz) apple juice*

*3 tablespoons lemon juice*

*1 tablespoon finely grated lemon rind*

*720 g (23 oz) caster sugar*

*¼ cup (60 ml/2 fl oz) brandy*

Cook apples in a saucepan with water over moderate heat until soft. Mash until smooth.

Combine mashed apples, apple juice, lemon juice and rind, sugar and brandy in a bowl.

Pour mixture into an ice cream maker. Follow the manufacturer's instructions.

**SERVES 6**

# MAPLE YOGHURT ICE

150 ml (5 fl oz) maple syrup
6 egg yolks
700 ml (21 fl oz) vanilla yoghurt

Simmer maple syrup in a small saucepan until thick.

Beat egg yolks in a bowl until thick and fluffy. Add maple syrup in a thin stream while still beating. Continue beating until cool. Whisk in yoghurt.

Pour into an ice cream maker. Follow the manufacturer's instructions.

**SERVES 6**

---

### MAPLE SYRUP

Maple syrup is a golden sweet liquid make by concentrating the sap of a sugar maple tree. It has a distinct flavour and is best known as a topping for pancakes.

---

# CHAMPAGNE AND BERRY GRANITA

185 g (6 oz) sugar
1½ cups (375 ml/12 fl oz) water
2 cups (500 ml/16 fl oz) champagne
500 g (1 lb) mixed berries

Stir sugar and water in a saucepan over low heat until sugar dissolves. Bring to the boil and boil for 2 minutes. Cool. Add champagne to sugar syrup.

Pour into a metal container and freeze for 2 to 3 hours, stirring every hour. Serve granita with berries.

**SERVES 6**

# VERY CHOCOLATE ICE CREAM

2 cups (500 ml/16 fl oz) milk
2 cups (500 ml/16 fl oz) cream
5 egg yolks
315 g (10 oz) sugar
90 g (3 oz) cocoa powder
125 g (4 oz) white chocolate, chopped
125 g (4 oz) milk chocolate, chopped

Heat cream and milk in a saucepan and bring to the boil. Beat egg yolks and sugar in a bowl until light and fluffy. When cream mixture boils, add cocoa and stir until smooth.

Whisk cream mixture into egg mixture. Fold through white and milk chocolate. Pour into an ice cream maker. Follow the manufacturer's instructions.

**SERVES 8**

# ZABAGLIONE ICE CREAM

This rich ice cream is ideal for an Italian meal.

4 egg yolks
185 g (6 oz) sugar
2 cups (500 ml/16 fl oz) milk
⅓ cup (80 ml/2½ fl oz) marsala

Place egg yolks and sugar in a bowl over a saucepan of boiling water. Beat until thick and creamy.

Add milk and stir until mixture forms a thin custard that coats the back of a spoon. Stir through marsala.

Pour mixture into an ice cream maker. Follow the manufacturer's instructions.

**SERVES 4**

# CARAMEL BANANA ICE CREAM

Caramel is available from good sweet or chocolate shops.

500 g (1 lb) ripe bananas
1½ tablespoons lemon juice
200 g (6½ oz) caster sugar
1 egg
¼ cup (60 ml/2 fl oz) milk
1¾ cups (450 ml/14 fl oz) cream
200 g (6½ oz) caramel, chopped

Process bananas, lemon juice and sugar in a food processor until smooth. Add egg, milk and cream. Process until just combined. Stir through caramel.

Pour into an ice cream maker. Follow the manufacturer's instructions.

**SERVES 6**

---

### STORING BANANAS

Always store bananas at room temperature. Never refrigerate or freeze them as they will turn black.

---

# Finishing Touches

*T*he difference between a great dessert and a show-stopper is often the finishing touches — that little something that defines your dessert as an extra special dish.

## Grated or Peeled Coconut

Pierce the coconut and pour out the liquid. Break the coconut open by tapping with a hammer around middle. Prise the meat out with a knife. Remove the skin with a vegetable peeler. Peel long strips with a vegetable peeler or grate in a food processor.

## Chocolate Strawberries

Melt chocolate of your choice and dip strawberries halfway into chocolate. Set and serve. An interesting variation is to use white chocolate first, let it set, then dip the berries into dark chocolate just a little shallower. This will give a striped effect.

## Strawberry Fans

Wash and dry strawberries, leaving the green stalk intact. Using a sharp knife, slice nearly all the way through each strawberry from the tip to the stalk. Gently fan out the slices.

*Pictured on previous pages: Citrus Curls, Chocolate Strawberries, Chocolate Macadamias, Chocolate Coffee Beans, Chocolate Shavings*

## Citrus Curls

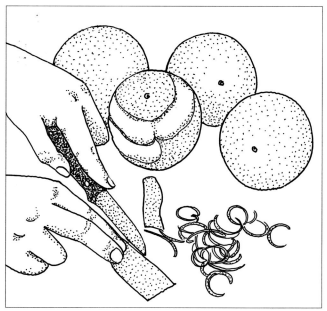

Cut strips of rind from oranges, limes and lemons. Place 125 g (4 oz) sugar in a saucepan with ¼ cup (60 ml/2 fl oz) water. Stir until sugar has dissolved. Bring to the boil and add rind strips. Cook for 3 to 4 minutes or until strips are tender. Drain on a wire rack and serve.

## Citrus Segments

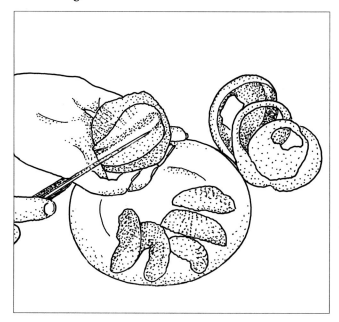

Peel all of the skin and white pith from the fruit. Using a sharp knife, cut down between the membranes and remove segments. Remove any pips.

## Basic Toffee Recipe

Place 250 g (8 oz) sugar and ½ cup (125 ml/4 fl oz) water in a small saucepan. Stir gently over low heat until sugar has dissolved. Use a wet pastry brush to brush sugar from the sides of the saucepan. Bring syrup to the boil and simmer until golden brown.

## Praline

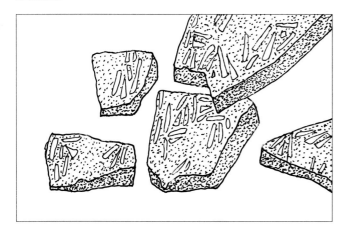

Make one quantity of toffee and pour over 90g (3 oz) slivered almonds in a greased baking tray. Allow to set and harden before breaking into pieces or placing in the food processor and processing into fine pieces. Further processing will result in praline powder.

## Sugar Bark

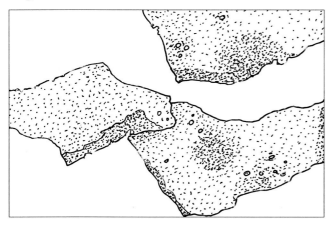

Sprinkle 3 tablespoons each of sugar, raw sugar and coffee sugar on a piece of foil. Place under the grill on low heat and cook until sugar melts. Remove from grill and allow to harden. Break into pieces to serve.

## Nut Clusters

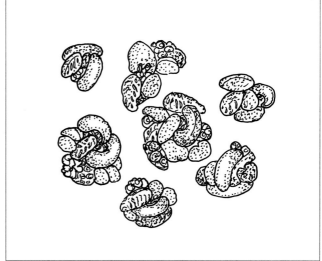

Make one quantity of toffee. Place small piles of nuts on a greased baking tray. Pour over a spoonful of toffee and cool until hard.

## Spun Toffee

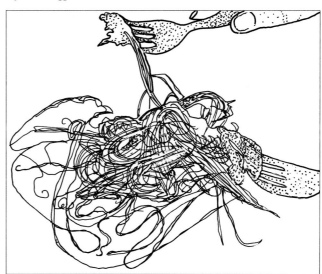

Make one quantity of toffee and allow to cool slightly. Dip a fork into the toffee and allow it to drip until a thin stream runs from the fork. Hold a long spatula or wooden spoon with your other hand. Quickly flick the fork back and forth over the spatula to form long, thin, toffee strands. Bunch the strands together and repeat the process. Note: Spun toffee breaks down very easily on humid or moist days. Make spun toffee close to serving time.

## Chocolate Curls

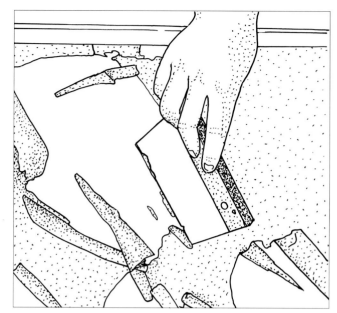

Melt chocolate in a small bowl over hot water. Pour the chocolate onto a cool, flat surface or a baking tray. Holding a scraper or spatula at a 45° angle, push against the chocolate to form chocolate curls.

## Chocolate Macadamias

Place chocolate in a small bowl and melt over simmering water. Place macadamias on a board and drizzle with chocolate.

*Praline, Spun Toffee, Nut Clusters, Sugar Bark*

## Chocolate Shapes

Make shapes — letters, flowers, hearts (any picture you like, really) — by piping melted chocolate onto greaseproof paper in the shape of your choice. Peel away carefully when set.

## Chocolate Leaves

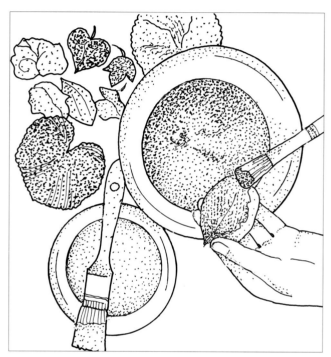

Wash and dry the leaves of your choice. Melt chocolate in a bowl over hot water. Paint the chocolate onto the underside of the leaves. When set, carefully peel the leaf away.

## Chocolate Coffee Beans

Melt the chocolate of your choice and dip coffee beans into chocolate. Set and serve.

# MEASURING MADE EASY

## HOW TO MEASURE DRY INGREDIENTS

| | | |
|---|---|---|
| 15 g | ½ oz | |
| 30 g | 1 oz | |
| 60 g | 2 oz | |
| 90 g | 3 oz | |
| 125 g | 4 oz | (¼ lb) |
| 155 g | 5 oz | |
| 185 g | 6 oz | |
| 220 g | 7 oz | |
| 250 g | 8 oz | (½ lb) |
| 280 g | 9 oz | |
| 315 g | 10 oz | |
| 345 g | 11 oz | |
| 375 g | 12 oz | (¾ lb) |
| 410 g | 13 oz | |
| 440 g | 14 oz | |
| 470 g | 15 oz | |
| 500 g | 16 oz | (1 lb) |
| 750 g | 24 oz | (1½ lb) |
| 1 kg | 32 oz | (2 lb) |

## QUICK CONVERSIONS

| | | |
|---|---|---|
| 5 mm | ¼ inch | |
| 1 cm | ½ inch | |
| 2 cm | ¾ inch | |
| 2.5 cm | 1 inch | |
| 5 cm | 2 inches | |
| 6 cm | 2½ inches | |
| 8 cm | 3 inches | |
| 10 cm | 4 inches | |
| 12 cm | 5 inches | |
| 15 cm | 6 inches | |
| 18 cm | 7 inches | |
| 20 cm | 8 inches | |
| 23 cm | 9 inches | |
| 25 cm | 10 inches | |
| 28 cm | 11 inches | |
| 30 cm | 12 inches | (1 foot) |
| 46 cm | 18 inches | |
| 50 cm | 20 inches | |
| 61 cm | 24 inches | (2 feet) |
| 77 cm | 30 inches | |

NOTE: We developed the recipes in this book in Australia where the tablespoon measure is 20 ml. In many other countries the tablespoon is 15 ml. For most recipes this difference will not be noticeable.

However, for recipes using baking powder, gelatine, bicarbonate of soda, small amounts of flour and cornflour, we suggest you add an extra teaspoon for each tablespoon specified.

Many people find it very convenient to use cup measurements. You can buy special measuring cups or measure water in an ordinary household cup to check it holds 250 ml (8 fl oz). This can then be used for both liquid and dry cup measurements.

## MEASURING LIQUIDS

### METRIC CUPS

| | | |
|---|---|---|
| ¼ cup | 60 ml | 2 fluid ounces |
| ⅓ cup | 80 ml | 2½ fluid ounces |
| ½ cup | 125 ml | 4 fluid ounces |
| ¾ cup | 180 ml | 6 fluid ounces |
| 1 cup | 250 ml | 8 fluid ounces |

### METRIC SPOONS

| | |
|---|---|
| ¼ teaspoon | 1.25 ml |
| ½ teaspoon | 2.5 ml |
| 1 teaspoon | 5 ml |
| 1 tablespoon | 20 ml |

## OVEN TEMPERATURES

| TEMPERATURES | CELSIUS (°C) | FAHRENHEIT (°F) | GAS MARK |
|---|---|---|---|
| Very Slow | 120 | 250 | ½ |
| Slow | 150 | 300 | 2 |
| Moderate | 160-180 | 325-350 | 3-4 |
| Moderately hot | 190-200 | 375-400 | 5-6 |
| Hot | 220-230 | 425-450 | 7-8 |
| Very hot | 250-260 | 475-500 | 9-10 |

Published by Murdoch Books®,
a division of Murdoch Magazines Pty Ltd,
213 Miller Street, North Sydney NSW 2060.

Chapter Opener and Front Cover Photography: Quentin Bacon.
Food Stylist: Donna Hay.
Food Stylist's Assistant: Jodie Vassallo.
Food Editor: Donna Hay.
Jacket Design: Sylvie Abecassis.
Front cover recipes: Lemon Meringue Pie (page 25),
Tangelo and Coconut Pudding (page 10), Berry Sauce (page 21).
Back cover recipes: Passionfruit Granita (page 79), Praline
Ice cream with Chocolate Fudge Sauce (page 83)

Managing Editor: Jane Price.
Food Editors: Kerrie Ray, Tracy Rutherford.
Publisher: Anne Wilson.
International Sales Manager: Mark Newman.

National Library of Australia Cataloguing-in-Publication Data:
Desserts, puddings & ices. Rev. ed. Includes index.
ISBN 0 86411 556 3. 1. Desserts. 2. Puddings. 3. Ice cream, ices, etc.
(Series: Bay Books cookery collection). 641.86.
First published in Australia in 1994. This edition first printed 1996.
Printed by Toppan Printing (S) Pte. Ltd, Singapore.

# Index